# A FLAT IRON FOR A FARTHING

## FARTHING

or, Some Passages in the Life of an only Son

## JULIANA HORATIA EWING

1st WORLD
LIBRARY
Literary Society

# A Flat Iron for a Farthing

## Juliana Horatia Ewing

© 1st World Library, 2007
PO Box 2211
Fairfield, IA 52556
www.1stworldlibrary.com
First Edition

LCCN: 2007930806

Softcover ISBN: 978-1-4218-4845-7
Hardcover ISBN: 978-1-4218-4748-1
eBook ISBN: 978-1-4218-4942-3

Purchase *"A Flat Iron for a Farthing"*
as a traditional bound book at:
www.1stWorldLibrary.com/purchase.asp?ISBN=978-1-4218-4845-7

1st World Library is a literary, educational organization
dedicated to:

- Creating a free internet library of downloadable ebooks

- Hosting writing competitions and offering book publishing
  scholarships.

Interested in more 1st World Library books? contact:
literacy@1stworldlibrary.com
Check us out at: www.1stworldlibrary.com

# 1<sup>st</sup> World Library Literary Society

## Giving Back to the World

"If you want to work on the core problem, it's early school literacy."

**- James Barksdale, former CEO of Netscape**

"No skill is more crucial to the future of a child, or to a democratic and prosperous society, than literacy."

**- Los Angeles Times**

"Literacy... means far more than learning how to read and write... The aim is to transmit... knowledge and promote social participation."

**- UNESCO**

"Literacy is not a luxury, it is a right and a responsibility. If our world is to meet the challenges of the twenty-first century we must harness the energy and creativity of all our citizens."

**- President Bill Clinton**

"Parents should be encouraged to read to their children, and teachers should be equipped with all available techniques for teaching literacy, so the varying needs and capacities of individual kids can be taken into account."

**- Hugh Mackay**

Dedicated

TO MY DEAR FATHER,

AND TO HIS SISTER, MY DEAR AUNT MARY,

IN MEMORY OF

THEIR GOOD FRIEND AND NURSE,

E. B.

OBIT 3 MARCH, 1872, AET. 83.

J. H. E.

## PREFACE

An apology is a sorry Preface to any book, however insignificant, and yet I am anxious to apologise for the title of this little tale. The story grew after the title had been (hastily) given, and so many other incidents gathered round the incident of the purchase of the flat iron as to make it no longer important enough to appear upon the title page. It would, however, be dishonest to change the name of a tale which is reprinted from a Magazine; and I can only apologise for an appearance of affectation in it which was not intended.

As the Dedication may seem to suggest that the character of Mrs. Bundle is a portrait, I may be allowed to say that, except in faithfulness, and tenderness, and high principle, she bears no likeness to my father's dear old nurse.

It may interest some of my child readers to know that the steep street and the farthing wares are real remembrances out of my own childhood. Though whether in these days of "advanced prices," the flat irons, the gridirons with the three fish upon them, and all those other valuable accessories to doll's housekeeping, which I once delighted to purchase, can still be obtained for a farthing each, I have lived too long out of the world of toys to be able to tell.

J. H. E.

# CONTENTS

# CHAPTER I

## MOTHERLESS

When the children clamour for a story, my wife says to me, "Tell them how you bought a flat iron for a farthing." Which I very gladly do; for three reasons. In the first place, it is about myself, and so I take an interest in it. Secondly, it is about some one very dear to me, as will appear hereafter. Thirdly, it is the only original story in my somewhat limited collection, and I am naturally rather proud of the favour with which it is invariably received. I think it was the foolish fancy of my dear wife and children combined that this most veracious history should be committed to paper. It was either because—being so unused to authorship—I had no notion of composition, and was troubled by a tyro tendency to stray from my subject; or because the part played by the flat iron, though important, was small; or because I and my affairs were most chiefly interesting to myself as writer, and my family as readers; or from a combination of all these reasons together, that my tale outgrew its first title and we had to add a second, and call it "Some Passages in the Life of an only Son."

Yes, I was an only son. I was an only child also, speaking as the world speaks, and not as Wordsworth's "simple child" spoke. But let me rather use the "little maid's" reckoning, and say that I have, rather than that I had, a sister. "Her grave is green, it may be seen." She peeped into the world, and we called her Alice; then she went away again and took my mother with her. It was my first great, bitter grief.

I remember well the day when I was led with much mysterious solemnity to see my new sister. She was then a week old.

"You must be quiet, sir," said Mrs. Bundle, a new member of our establishment, "and not on no account make no noise to disturb your dear, pretty mamma."

Repressed by this accumulation of negatives, as well as by the size and dignity of Mrs. Bundle's outward woman, I went a-tiptoe under her large shadow to see my new acquisition.

Very young children are not always pretty, but my sister was beautiful beyond the wont of babies. It is an old simile, but she was like a beautiful painting of a cherub. Her little face wore an expression seldom seen except on a few faces of those who have but lately come into this world, or those who are about to go from it. The hair that just gilded the pink head I was allowed to kiss was one shade paler than that which made a great aureole on the pillow about the pale face of my "dear, pretty" mother.

Years afterwards—in Belgium—I bought an old mediaeval painting of a Madonna. That Madonna had a stiffness, a deadly pallor, a thinness of face incompatible with strict beauty. But on the thin lips there was a smile for which no word is lovely enough; and in the eyes was a pure and far-seeing look, hardly to be imagined except by one who painted (like Fra Angelico) upon his knees. The background (like that of many religious paintings of the date) was gilt. With such a look and such a smile my mother's face shone out of the mass of her golden hair the day she died. For this I bought the picture; for this I keep it still.

But to go back.

I liked Mrs. Bundle. I had taken to her from the evening when she arrived in a red shawl, with several bandboxes. My affection for her was established next day, when she washed my face before dinner. My own nurse was bony, her hands were all knuckles, and she washed my face as she scrubbed the nursery floor on Saturdays. Mrs. Bundle's plump palms were like pincushions, and she washed my face as if it had been a baby's.

On the evening of the day when I first saw Sister Alice, I took tea in the housekeeper's room. My nurse was out for the evening, but Mrs. Cadman from the village was of the party, and neither cakes nor conversation flagged. Mrs. Cadman had hollow eyes, and (on occasion) a hollow voice, which was very impressive. She wore curl-papers continually, which once caused me to ask my nurse if she ever took them out.

"On Sundays she do," said Nurse.

"She's very religious then, I suppose," said I; and I did really think it a great compliment that she paid to the first day of the week.

I was only just four years old at this time—an age when one is apt to ask inconvenient questions and to make strange observations—when one is struggling to understand life through the mist of novelties about one, and the additional confusion of falsehood which it is so common to speak or to insinuate without scruple to very young children.

The housekeeper and Mrs. Cadman had conversed for some

time after tea without diverting my attention from the new box of bricks which Mrs. Bundle (commissioned by my father) had brought from the town for me; but when I had put all the round arches on the pairs of pillars, and had made a very successful "Tower of Babel" with cross layers of the bricks tapering towards the top, I had leisure to look round and listen.

"I never know'd one with that look as lived," Mrs. Cadman was saying, in her hollow tone. "It took notice from the first. Mark my words, ma'am, a sweeter child I never saw, but it's *too* good and *too* pretty to be long for this world."

It is difficult to say exactly how much one understands at four years old, or rather how far one quite comprehends the things one perceives in part. I understood, or felt, enough of what I heard, and of the sympathetic sighs that followed Mrs. Cadman's speech, to make me stumble over the Tower of Babel, and present myself at Mrs. Cadman's knee with the question—

"Is mamma too pretty and good for this world, Mrs. Cadman?"

I caught her elderly wink as quickly as the housekeeper, to whom it was directed. I was not completely deceived by her answer.

"Why, bless his dear heart, Master Reginald. Who did he think I was talking about, love?"

"My new baby sister," said I, without hesitation.

"No such thing, lovey," said the audacious Mrs. Cadman; "housekeeper and me was talking about Mrs. Jones's little boy."

"Where does Mrs. Jones live?" I asked.

"In London town, my dear."

I sighed. I knew nothing of London town, and could not prove that Mrs. Jones had no existence. But I felt dimly dissatisfied, in spite of a slice of sponge-cake, and being put to bed (for a treat) in papa's dressing-room. My sleep was broken by uneasy dreams, in which Mrs. Jones figured with the face of Mrs. Cadman and her hollow voice. I had a sensation that that night the house never went to rest. People came in and out with a pretentious purpose of not awaking me. My father never came to bed. I felt convinced that I heard the doctor's voice in the passage. At last, while it was yet dark, and when I seemed to have been sleeping and waking, waking and falling asleep again in my crib for weeks, my father came in with a strange look upon his face, and took me up in his arms, and wrapped a blanket round me, saying mamma wanted to kiss me, but I must be very good and make no noise. There was little fear of that! I gazed in utter silence at the sweet face that was whiter than the sheet below it, the hair that shone brighter than ever in the candlelight. Only when I kissed her, and she had laid her wan hand on my head, I whispered to my father, "Why is mamma so cold?"

With a smothered groan he carried me back to bed, and I cried myself to sleep. It was too true, then. She was too good and too pretty for this world, and before sunrise she was gone.

Before the day was ended Sister Alice left us also. She never knew a harder resting-place than our mother's arms.

## CHAPTER II

## "THE LOOK"—RUBENS—MRS. BUNDLE AGAIN

My widowed father and I were both terribly lonely. The depths of his loss in the lovely and lovable wife who had been his constant companion for nearly six years I could not fathom at the time. For my own part, I was quite as miserable as I have ever been since, and I doubt if I shall ever feel such overwhelming desolation again, unless the same sorrow befalls me as then befell him.

I "fretted"—as the servants expressed it—to such an extent as to affect my health; and I fancy it was because my father's attention was called to the fact that I was fast fading after the mother and sister whose death (and my own loneliness) I bewailed, that he roused himself from his own grief to comfort mine. Once more I was "dressed" after tea. Of late my bony nurse had not thought it necessary to go through this ceremony, and I had crept about in the same crape-covered frock from breakfast to bedtime.

Now I came down to dessert again, and though I think the empty place at the end of the table gave my father a fresh shock when I took my old post by him, yet I fancy the lonely evening was less lonely for my presence.

Juliana Horatia Ewing

From his intense indulgence I think I dimly gathered that he thought me ill. I combined this in my mind with a speech of my nurse's that I had overheard, and which gave me the horrors at the time—"He's got *the look*! It's his poor ma over again!"—and I felt a sort of melancholy self-importance not uncommon with children who are out of health.

I may say here that my nurse had a quality very common amongst uneducated people. She was "sensational;" and her custom of going over all the circumstances of my mother's death and funeral (down to the price of the black paramatta of which her own dress was composed) with her friends, when she took me out walking, had not tended to make me happier or more cheerful.

That night I ate more from my father's plate than I had eaten for weeks. As I lay after dinner with my head upon his breast, he stroked my curls with a tender touch that seemed to heal my griefs, and said, almost in a tone of remorse,

"What can papa do for you, my poor dear boy?"

I looked up quickly into his face.

"What would Regie like?" he persisted.

I quite understood him now, and spoke out boldly the desires of my heart.

"Please, papa, I should like Mrs. Bundle for a nurse; and I do very much want Rubens."

"And who is Rubens?" asked my father.

"Oh, please, it's a dog," I said. "It belongs to Mr. Mackenzie at the school. And it's such a little dear, all red and white;

and it licked my face when nurse and I were there yesterday, and I put my hand in its mouth, and it rolled over on its back, and it's got long ears, and it followed me all the way home, and I gave it a piece of bread, and it can sit up, and"—

"But, my little man," interrupted my father—and he had absolutely smiled at my catalogue of marvels—"if Rubens belongs to Mr. Mackenzie, and is such a wonderful fellow, I'm afraid Mr. Mackenzie won't part with him."

"He would," I said, "but—" and I paused, for I feared the barrier was insurmountable.

"But what?" said my father.

"He wants ten shillings for him, Nurse says."

"If that's all, Regie," said my father, "you and I will go and buy Rubens to-morrow morning."

Rubens was a little red and white spaniel of much beauty and sagacity. He was the prettiest, gentlest, most winning of playfellows. With him by my side, I now ran merrily about, instead of creeping moodily at the heels of nurse and her friends. Abundantly occupied in testing the tricks he knew, and teaching him new ones, I had the less leisure to listen open-mouthed to cadaverous gossip of the Cadman class. Finally, when I had bidden him good-night a hundred times, with absolutely fraternal embraces, I was soothed by the light weight of his head resting on my foot. He seemed to chase the hideous fancies which had hitherto passed from nurse's daytime conversation to trouble my night visions, as he would chase a water-fowl from a reedy marsh, and I slept—as he did—peacefully.

Nor was this all. My other wish was also to be fulfilled, but not without some vexations beforehand. It was by a certain air and tone which my nurse suddenly assumed towards me, and which it is difficult to describe by any other word than "heighty-teighty," and also by dark hints of changes which she hoped (but seemed far from believing) would be for my good, and finally, by downright lamentations and tragic inquiries as to what she had done to be parted from her boy, and "could her chickabiddy have the heart to drive away his loving and faithful nursey," that I learned that it was contemplated to supersede her by some one else, and that if she did not know that I was to blame in the matter, she at any rate believed me to have influence enough to obtain a reversal of the decree. That Mrs. Bundle was to be her successor I gathered from allusions to "your great fat bouncing women that would eat their heads off; but as to cleaning out a nursery—let them see!" But her most masterly stroke was a certain conversation with Mrs. Cadman carried on in my hearing.

"Have you ever notice, Mrs. Cadman," inquired my bony nurse of her not less bony visitor—"Have you ever notice how them stout people as looks so good-natured as if butter wouldn't melt in their mouths is that wicked and cruel underneath?" And then followed a series of nurse's most ghastly anecdotes, relative to fat mothers who had ill-treated their children, fat nurses who had nearly been the death of their unfortunate charges, fat female murderers, and a fat acquaintance of her own, who was "taken" in apoplexy after a fit of rage with her husband.

"What a warning! what a moral!" said Mrs. Cadman. She meant it for a pious observation, but I felt that the warning and the moral were for me. And not even the presence of Rubens could dispel the darkness of my dreams that night.

Alternately goaded and caressed by my nurse, who now laid

aside a habit she had of beating a tattoo with her knuckles on my head when I was naughty, to the intense confusion and irritation of my brain, I at last resolved to beg my father to let her remain with us. I felt that it was—as she had pointed out—intense ingratitude on my part to wish to part with her, and I said as much when I went down to dessert that evening. Morever, I now lived in vague fear of those terrible qualities which lay hidden beneath Mrs. Bundle's benevolent exterior.

"If nurse has been teasing you about the matter," said my father, with a frown, "that would decide me to get rid of her, if I had not so decided before. As to your not liking Mrs. Bundle now—My dear little son, you must learn to know your own mind. You told me you wanted Mrs. Bundle—by very good luck I have been able to get hold of her, and when she comes you must make the best of her."

She came the next day, and my bony nurse departed. She wept indignantly, I wept remorsefully, and then waited in terror for the manifestation of Mrs. Bundle's cruel propensities.

I waited in vain. The reign of Mrs. Bundle was a reign of peace and plenty, of loving-kindness and all good things. Moreover it was a reign of wholesomeness, both for body and mind. She did not give me cheese and beer from her own supper when she was in a good temper, nor pound my unfortunate head with her knuckles if I displeased her. She was strict in the maintenance of a certain old-fashioned nursery etiquette, which obliged me to put away my chair after meals, fold my clothes at bedtime, put away my toys when I had done with them, say "please," "thank you," grace before and after meals, prayers night and morning, a hymn in bed, and the Church Catechism on Sunday. She snubbed the maids who alluded in my presence to things I could not or should not understand, and she directed her own conversation to me, on matters suitable to my age, instead of talking over my childish head to her gossips. The stories of horror and crime, the fore-doomed babies, the murders, the mysterious whispered communications faded from my untroubled brain. Nurse Bundle's tales were of the young masters and misses she had known. Her worst domestic tragedy was about the boy who broke his leg over the chair he had failed to put away after breakfast. Her romances were the good old Nursery Legends of Dick Whittington, the Babes in the Wood, and so forth. My dreams became less like the columns of a provincial newspaper. I imagined myself another Marquis of Carabas, with Rubens in boots. I made a desert island in the garden, which only lacked the geography-book peculiarity of "water all round" it. I planted beans in the fond hope that they would tower to the skies and take me with them. I became—in fancy—Lord Mayor of London, and Mrs. Bundle shared my civic throne and dignities, and we gave Rubens six beefeaters and a barge to wait upon his pleasure.

Life, in short, was utterly changed for me. I grew strong, and stout, and well, and happy. And I loved Nurse Bundle.

# CHAPTER III

## THE DARK LADY—TROUBLE IMPENDING— BEAUTIFUL, GOLDEN MAMMA

So two years passed away. Nurse Bundle was still with me. With her I "did lessons" after a fashion. I learned to read, I had many of the Psalms and a good deal of poetry—sacred and secular—by heart. In an old-fashioned, but slow and thorough manner, I acquired the first outlines of geography, arithmetic, etc., and what Mrs. Bundle taught me I repeated to Rubens. But I don't think he ever learned the "capital towns of Europe," though we studied them together under the same oak tree.

We had a happy two years of it together under the Bundle dynasty, and then trouble came.

I was never fond of demonstrative affection from strangers. The ladies who lavish kisses and flattery upon one's youthful head after eating papa's good dinner—keeping a sharp protective eye on their own silk dresses, and perchance pricking one with a brooch or pushing a curl into one eye with a kid-gloved finger—I held in unfeigned abhorrence. But over and above my natural instinct against the unloving fondling of drawing-room visitors, I had a special and peculiar antipathy to Miss Eliza Burton.

At first, I think I rather admired her. Her rolling eyes, the black hair plastered low upon her forehead,—the colour high, but never changeable or delicate—the amplitude and rustle of her skirts, the impressiveness of her manner, her very positive matureness, were just what the crude taste of childhood is apt to be fascinated by. She was the sister of my father's man of business; and she and her brother were visiting at my home. She really looked well in the morning, "toned down" by a fresh, summer muslin, and all womanly anxiety to relieve my father of the trouble of making the tea for breakfast.

"Dear Mr. Dacre, *do* let me relieve you of that task," she cried, her ribbons fluttering over the sugar-basin. "I never like to see a gentleman sacrificing himself for his guests at breakfast. You have enough to do at dinner, carving large joints, and jointing those terrible birds. At breakfast a gentleman should have no trouble but the cracking of his own egg and the reading of his own newspaper. Now do let me!"

Miss Burton's long fingers were almost on the tea-caddy; but at that moment my father quietly opened it, and began to measure out the tea.

"I never trouble my lady visitors with this," he said, quietly. "I am only too well accustomed to it."

Child as I was, I felt well satisfied that my father would let no one fill my mother's place. For so it was, and all Miss Burton's efforts failed to put her, even for a moment, at the head of his table.

I do not quite know how or when it was that I began to realize that such was her effort. I remember once hearing a scrap of conversation between our most respectable and respectful butler and the housekeeper—"behind the scenes"—as the former worthy came from the breakfast-room.

"And how's the new missis this morning, Mr. Smith?" asked the housekeeper, with a bitterness not softened by the prospect of possible dethronement.

"Another try for the tea-tray, ma'am," replied Smith, "but it's no go."

"A brazen, black-haired old maid!" cried the housekeeper. "To think of her taking the place of that sweet angel, Mrs. Dacre (and she barely two years in her grave), and pretending to act a mother's part by the poor boy and all. I've no patience!"

On one excuse or another, the Burtons contrived to extend their visit; and the prospect of a marriage between my father and Miss Burton was now discussed too openly behind his back for me to fail to hear it. Then Nurse Bundle on this subject hardly exercised her usual discretion in withholding me from servants' gossip, and servants' gossip from me. Her own indignation was strongly aroused, and I had no difficulty in connecting her tearful embraces, and her allusions to my dead mother, with the misfortune we all believed to be impending.

At first I had admired Miss Burton's bouncing looks. Then my head had been turned to some extent by her flattery, and by the establishment of that most objectionable of domestic jokes, the parody of love affairs in connection with children. Miss Burton called me her little sweetheart, and sent me messages, and vowed that I was quite a little man of the world, and then was sure that I was a desperate flirt. The lank lawyer wagged my hand of a morning, and said, "And how is Miss Eliza's little beau?" And I laughed, and looked important, and talked rather louder, and escaped as often as I could from the nursery, and endeavoured to act up to the character assigned me with about as much grace as AEsop's donkey trying to dance. I must have become a perfect nuisance to any sensible person at this period, and indeed my father had an interview with Nurse Bundle on the subject.

"Master Reginald seems to me to be more troublesome than he used to be, nurse," said my father.

"Indeed you say true, sir," said Mrs. Bundle, only too glad to reply; "but it's the drawing-room and not the nursery as does it. Miss Burton is always a begging for him to be allowed to stay up at nights and to lunch in the dining-room, and to come down of a morning, and to have a half-holiday in an afternoon; and, saving your better knowledge, sir, it's a bad thing to break into the regular ways of children. It ain't for their happiness, nor for any one else's."

"You are perfectly right, perfectly right," said my father, "and it shall not occur again. Ah! my poor boy," he added in an irrepressible outburst, "you suffer for lack of a mother's care. I do what I can, but a man cannot supply a woman's place to a child."

Mrs. Bundle's feelings at this soliloquy may be imagined. "You might have knocked me down with a feather, sir," she assured the butler (unlikely as it seemed!) in describing the scene afterwards. She found strength, however, to reply to my father's remark.

"Indeed, sir, a mother's place never can be filled to a child by no one whatever. Least of all such a mother as he had in your dear lady. But he's a boy, sir, and not a girl, and in all reason a father is what he'll chiefly look to in a year or two. And for the meanwhile, sir, I ask you, could Master Reginald look better or behave better than he did afore the company come?

It's only natural as smart ladies who knows nothing whatever of children, and how they should be brought up, and what's for their good, should think it a kindness to spoil them. Any one may see the lady has no notion of children, and would be the ruin of Master Reginald if she had much to do with him; but when the company's gone, sir, and he's left quiet with his papa, you'll find him as good as any young gentleman needs to be, if you'll excuse my freedom in speaking, sir."

Whatever my father thought of Mrs. Bundle's freedom of speech, he only said,

"Master Reginald will be quite under your orders for the future, Nurse," and so dismissed her.

And Mrs. Bundle having "said her say," withdrew to say it over again in confidence to the housekeeper.

As for me, if my vanity was stronger than my good taste for a while, the quickness of childish instinct soon convinced me that Miss Burton had no real affection for me. Then I was puzzled by her spasmodic attentions when my father was in the room, and her rough repulses when I "bothered" her at less appropriate moments. I got tired of her, too, of the sound of her voice, of her black hair and unchanging red cheeks. And from the day that I caught her beating Rubens for lying on the edge of her dress, I lived in terror of her. Those rolling black eyes had not a pleasant look when the lady was out of temper. And was she really to be the new mistress of the house? To take the place of my fair, gentle, beautiful mother? That wave of household gossip which for ever surges behind the master's back was always breaking over me now, in expressions of pity for the motherless child of "the dear lady dead and gone."

"I don't like black hair," I announced one day at luncheon; "I like beautiful, shining, golden hair, like poor mamma's."

"Don't talk nonsense, Reginald," said my father, angrily, and shortly afterwards I was dismissed to the nursery.

If I had only had my childish memory to trust to, I do not think that I could have kept so clear a remembrance of my mother as I had. But in my father's dressing-room there hung a water-colour sketch of his young wife, with me—her first baby—on her lap. It was a very happy portrait. The little one was nestled in her arms, and she herself was just looking up with a bright smile of happiness and pride. That look came full at the spectator, and perhaps it was because it was so very lifelike that I had (ever since I could remember) indulged a curious freak of childish sentiment by nodding to the picture and saying, "Good-morning, mamma," whenever I came into the room. Such little superstitions become part of one's life, and I freely confess that I salute that portrait still! I remember, too, that as time went on I lost sight of the fact that it was I who lay on my mother's lap, and always regarded the two as Mamma and Sister Alice—that ever-baby sister whom I had once kissed, and no more. I generally saw them at least once a day, for it was my privilege to play in my father's dressing-room during part of his toilet, and we had a stereotyped joke between us in reference to his shaving, which always ended in my receiving a piece of the creamy lather on the tip of my nose.

But it was one evening when the shadow hanging over the household was deepest upon me, that I slipped unobserved out of the drawing-room where Miss Burton was "performing" on my mother's piano, and crept slowly and sadly upstairs. I went slowly, partly out of my heavy grief, and partly because I carried Rubens in my arms. Had not the lawyer kicked him because he lay upon the pedal? I was resolved that after such an insult he should not so much as have the trouble of walking upstairs. So I carried him, and as I went I condoled with him.

"Did the nasty man kick him? My poor Ru, my darling, dear Ru! The pedal is yours, and not his, and the whole house is yours, and not his nor Miss Burton's; and oh, I wish they would go!"

As I whined, Rubens whined; as I kissed him he licked me, and the result was unfavourable to balance, and I was obliged to sit down on a step. And as I sat I wept, and as I wept that overpowering mother-need came over me, which drives even the little ragamuffin of the gutter to carry his complaints to "mother" for comfort and redress. And I took up Rubens in my arms again, sobbing, and saying, "I shall go to Mamma!" and so weeping and in the darkness we crept into the dressing-room.

I could see nothing, but I knew well where "Mamma" was, and standing under the picture, I sobbed out my incoherent complaint.

"Good-evening, Mamma! Good-evening, Sister Alice! Please, Mamma, it's me and Rubens." (Sobs on my part, and frantic attempts by Rubens to lick every inch of my face at once.) "And please, Mamma, we're very miser-r-r-rable. And oh! please, Mamma, don't let papa marry Miss Burton. Please, please don't, dear, beautiful, golden Mamma! And oh! how we wish you could come back! Rubens and I."

My voice died away with a wail which was dismally echoed by Rubens. Then, suddenly, in the darkness came a sob that was purely human, and I was clasped in a woman's arms, and covered with tender kisses and soothing caresses. For one wild moment, in my excitement, and the boundless faith of childhood, I thought my mother had heard me, and come back.

But it was only Nurse Bundle. She had been putting away some clothes in my father's bedroom, and had been drawn to the dressing-room by hearing my voice.

I think this scene decided her to take some active steps. I feel convinced that in some way it was through her influence that a letter of invitation was despatched the following day to Aunt Maria.

# CHAPTER IV

## AUNT MARIA—THE ENEMY ROUTED—
## LONDON TOWN

Aunt Maria was my father's sister. She was married to a wealthy gentleman, and had a large family of children. It was from her that we originally got Nurse Bundle; and anecdotes of her and of my cousins, and wonderful accounts of London (where they lived), had long figured conspicuously in Mrs. Bundle's nursery chronicles.

Aunt Maria came, and Uncle Ascott came with her.

It is not altogether without a reason that I speak of them in this order. Aunt Maria was the active partner of their establishment. She was a clever, vigorous, well-educated, inartistic, kindly, managing woman. She was not exactly "meddling," but when she thought it her duty to interfere in a matter, no delicacy of scruples, and no nervousness baulked the directness of her proceedings. When she was most sweeping or uncompromising, Uncle Ascott would say, "My dear Maria!" But it was generally from a spasm of nervous cowardice, and not from any deliberate wish to interrupt Aunt Maria's course of action. He trusted her entirely.

Aunt Maria was very shrewd, and that long interview with

Nurse Bundle in her own room was hardly needed to acquaint her with the condition of domestic politics in our establishment. She "took in" the Burtons with one glance. The ladies "fell out" the following evening. The Burtons left Dacrefield the next morning, and at lunch Aunt Maria "pulled them to pieces" with as little remorse as a cook would pluck a partridge. I never saw Miss Eliza Burton again.

Aunt Maria did not fondle or spoil me. She might perhaps have shown more tenderness to her brother's only and motherless child; but, after Miss Burton, hers was a fault on the right side. She had a kindly interest in me, and she showed it by asking me to pay her a visit in London.

"It will do the child good, Regie," she said to my father. "He will be with other children, and all our London sights will be new to him. I will take every care of him, and you must come up and fetch him back. It will do you good too."

"To be sure!" chimed in Uncle Ascott, patting me good-naturedly on the head; "Master Reginald will fancy himself in Fairy Land. There are the Zoological Gardens, and Madame Tussaud's Waxwork Exhibition, and the Pantomime, and no one knows what besides! We shall make him quite at home! He and Helen are just the same age, I think, and Polly's a year or so younger, eh, mamma?"

"Nineteen months," said Aunt Maria, decisively; and she turned once more to my father, upon whom she was urging certain particulars.

It was with unfeigned joy that I heard my father say,

"Well, thank you, Maria. I do think it will do him good. And I'll certainly come and look you and Robert up myself."

There was only one drawback to my pleasure, when the much anticipated time of my first visit to London came. Aunt Maria did not like dogs; Uncle Ascott too said that "they were very rural and nice for the country, but that they didn't do in a town house. Besides which, Regie," he added, "such a pretty dog as Rubens would be sure to be stolen. And you wouldn't like that."

"I will take good care of Rubens, my boy," added my father; and with this promise I was obliged to content myself.

The excitement and pleasure of the various preparations for my visit were in themselves a treat. There had been some domestic discussion as to a suitable box for my clothes, and the matter was not quickly settled. There happened to be no box of exactly the convenient size in the house, and it was proposed to pack my things with Nurse Bundle's in one of the larger cases. This was a disappointment to my dignity; and I ventured to hint that I "should like a trunk all to myself, like a grown-up gentleman," without, however, much hope that my wishes would be fulfilled. The surprise was all the pleasanter when, on the day before our departure, there arrived by the carrier's cart from our nearest town a small, daintily-finished trunk, with a lock and key to it, and my initials in brass nails upon the outside. It was a parting gift from my father.

"I like young ladies and gentlemen to have things nice about 'em," Nurse Bundle observed, as we prepared to pack my trunk. "Then they takes a pride in their things, and so it stands to reason they takes more care of 'em."

To this excellent sentiment I gave my heartiest assent, and proceeded to illustrate it by the fastidious care with which I selected and folded the clothes I wished to take. As I examined my socks for signs of wear and tear, and then

Juliana Horatia Ewing

folded them by the ingenious process of grasping the heels and turning them inside out, in imitation of Nurse Bundle, an idea struck me, based upon my late reading and approaching prospects of travel.

"Nurse," said I, "I think I should like to learn to darn socks, because, you know, I might want to know how, if I was cast away on a desert island."

"If ever you find yourself on a desolate island, Master Reginald," said Nurse Bundle, "just you write straight off to me, and I'll come and do them kind of things for you."

"Well," said I, "only mind you bring Rubens, if I haven't got him."

For I had dim ideas that some Robinson Crusoe adventures might befall me before I returned home from this present expedition.

My father's place was about sixty miles from London. Mr. and Mrs. Ascott had come down in their own carriage, and were to return the same way.

I was to go with them, and Nurse Bundle also. She was to sit in the rumble of the carriage behind. Every particular of each new arrangement afforded me great amusement; and I could hardly control my impatience for the eventful day to arrive.

It came at last. There was very early breakfast for us all in the dining-room. No appetite, however, had I; and very cruel I thought Aunt Maria for insisting that I should swallow a certain amount of food, as a condition of being allowed to go at all. My enforced breakfast over, I went to look for Rubens. Ever since the day when it was first settled that I should go, the dear dog had kept close, very close at my heels. That depressed and aimless wandering about which always afflicts the dogs of the household when any of the family are going away from home was strong upon him. After the new trunk came into my room, Rubens took into his head a fancy for lying upon it; and though the brass nails must have been very uncomfortable, and though my bed was always free to him, on the box he was determined to be, and on the box he lay for hours together.

It was on the box that I found him, in the portico, despite the cords which now added a fresh discomfort to his self-chosen resting-place. I called to him, but though he wagged his tail he seemed disinclined to move, and lay curled up with one eye shut and one fixed on the carriage at the door.

"He's been trying to get into the carriage, sir," said the butler.

"You want to go too, poor Ruby, don't you?" I said; and I went in search of meats to console him.

He accepted a good breakfast from my hands with gratitude, and then curled himself up with one eye watchful as before. The reason of his proceedings was finally made evident by his determined struggles to accompany us at the last; and it was not till he had been forcibly shut up in the coach-house that we were able to start. My grief at parting with him was lessened by the distraction of another question.

Of all places about our equipage, I should have preferred riding with the postilion. Short of that, I was most anxious to sit behind in the rumble with my nurse. This favour was at length conceded, and after a long farewell from my father, gilded with a sovereign in my pocket, I was, with a mountain of wraps, consigned to the care of Nurse Bundle in the back seat.

The dew was still on the ground, the birds sang their loudest, the morning air was fresh and delicious, and before we had driven five miles on our way I could have eaten three such breakfasts as the one I had rejected at six o'clock. In the first two villages through which we drove people seemed to be only just getting up and beginning the day's business. In one or two "genteel" houses the blinds were still down; in reference to which I resolved that when *I* grew up I would not waste the best part of the day in bed, with the sun shining, the birds singing, the flowers opening, and country people going about their business, all beyond my closed windows.

"Nurse, please, I should like always to have breakfast at six o'clock. Do you hear, Nursey?" I added, for Mrs. Bundle feigned to be absorbed in contemplating a flock of sheep which were being driven past us.

"Very well, my dear. We'll see."

That "we'll see" of Nurse Bundle's was a sort of moral soothing-syrup which she kept to allay inconvenient curiosity and over-pertinacious projects in the nursery.

I had soon reason to decide that if I had breakfast at six, luncheon would not be unacceptable at half-past ten, at about which time I lost sight of the scenery and confined my attention to a worsted workbag in which Nurse Bundle had a store of most acceptable buns. Halting shortly after this to water the horses, a glass of milk was got for me from a wayside inn, over the door of which hung a small gate, on whose bars the following legend was painted:—

"This gate hangs well
And hinders none.
Refresh and pay,
And travel on."

"Did you put that up?" I inquired of the man who brought my milk.

"No, sir. It's been there long enough," was his reply.

"What does 'hinders none' mean?" I asked.

The man looked back, and considered the question.

"It means as it's not in the way of nothing. It don't hinder nobody," he replied at last.

"It couldn't if it wanted to," said I; "for it doesn't reach across the road. If it did, I suppose it would be a tollbar."

"He's a rum little chap, that!" said the waiter to Nurse Bundle, when he had taken back my empty glass. And he unmistakably nodded at me.

"What is a rum little chap, Nurse?" I inquired when we had fairly started once more.

"It's very low language," said Mrs. Bundle, indignantly; and this fact depressed me for several miles.

At about half-past eleven we rattled into Farnham, and stopped to lunch at "The Bush." I was delighted to get down from my perch, and to stretch my cramped legs by running about in the charming garden behind that celebrated inn. Dim bright memories are with me still of the long-windowed parlour opening into a garden verdant with grass, and stately yew hedges, and formal clipped trees; gay, too, with bright flowers, and mysterious with a walk winding under an arch of the yew hedge to the more distant bowling-green. On one side of this arch an admirably-carved stone figure in broadcoat and ruffles played perpetually upon a stone fiddle to an equally spirited shepherdess in hoop and high heels, who was for ever posed in dancing posture upon her pedestal and never danced away. As I wandered round the garden whilst luncheon was being prepared, I was greatly taken with these figures, and wondered if it might be that they were an enchanted prince and princess turned to stone by some wicked witch, envious of their happiness in the peaceful garden amid the green alleys and fragrant flowers. As I ate my luncheon I felt as if I were consuming what was their property, and pondered the supposition that some day the spell might be broken, and the stone-bound couple came down from those high pedestals, and go dancing and fiddling into the Farnham streets.

They showed no symptoms of moving whilst we remained, and, duly refreshed, we now proceeded on our way. I rejected the offer of a seat inside the carriage with scorn, and Nurse and I clambered back to our perch. No easy matter for either of us, by the way!—Nurse Bundle being so much too large, and I so much too small, to compass the feat with anything approaching to ease.

I was greatly pleased with the dreary beauties of Bagshot Heath, and Nurse Bundle (to whom the whole journey was familiar) enlivened this part of our way by such anecdotes of Dick Turpin, the celebrated highwayman, as she deemed suitable for my amusement. With what interest I gazed at the little house by the roadside where Turpin was wont to lodge, and where, arriving late one night, he demanded beef-steak for supper in terms so peremptory that, there being none in the house, the old woman who acted as his housekeeper was obliged to walk, then and there, to the nearest town to procure it! This and various other incidents of the robber's career I learned from Nurse Bundle, who told me that traditions of his exploits and character were still fresh in the neighbouring villages.

At Virginia Water we dined and changed horses. We stayed here longer than was necessary, that I might see the lake and the ship; and Uncle Ascott gave sixpence to an old man with a wooden leg who told us all about it. And still I declined an inside place, and went back with Nurse Bundle to the rumble. Early rising and the long drive began to make me sleepy. The tame beauties of the valley of the Thames drew little attention from my weary eyes; and I do not remember much about the place where we next halted, except that the tea tasted of hay, and that the bread and butter were good.

I gazed dreamily at Hounslow, despite fresh tales of Dick Turpin; and all the successive "jogs" by which Nurse called my incapable attention to the lamplighters, the shops, the bottles in the chemists' windows, and Hyde Park, failed to rouse me to any intelligent appreciation of the great city, now that I had reached it. After a long weary dream of rattle and bustle, and dim lamps, and houses stretching upwards like Jack's beanstalk through the chilly and foggy darkness, the carriage stopped with one final jolt in a quiet and partially-lighted square; and I was lifted down, and staggered into a house where the light was as abundant and overpowering as it was feeble and inefficient without, and, cramped in my limbs, and smothered with shawls, I could only beg in my utter weariness to be put to bed.

Aunt Maria was always sensible, and generally kind.

"Bring him at once to his room, Mrs. Bundle," she said, "and get his clothes off, and I will bring him some hot wine and water and a few rusks." As in a dream, I was undressed, my face and hands washed, my prayers said in a somewhat perfunctory fashion, and my evening hymn commuted in consideration of my fatigues for the beautiful verse, "I will lay me down in peace, and take my rest," etc.; and by the time that I sank luxuriously between the clean sheets, I was almost sufficiently restored to appreciate the dainty appearance of my room. Then Aunt Maria brought me the hot wine and water flavoured with sleep-giving cloves, and Nurse folded my clothes, and tucked me up, and left me, with the friendly reflection of the lamps without to keep me company.

I do not think I had really been to sleep, but I believe I was dozing, when I fancied that I heard the familiar sound of Rubens lapping water from the toilette jug in my room at home. Just conscious that I was not there, and that Rubens could not be here, the sound began to trouble me. At first I was too sleepy to care to look round. Then as I became more awake and the sound not less distinct, I felt fidgety and frightened, and at last called faintly for Nurse Bundle.

Then the sound stopped. I could hardly breathe, and had just resolved upon making a brave sally for assistance, when— plump! *something* alighted on my bed, and, wildly impossible as it seemed, Rubens himself waggled up to my pillow, and began licking my face as if his life depended on laying my nose and all other projecting parts of my countenance flat with my cheeks.

How he had got to London we never knew. As he made an easy escape from the coach-house at Dacrefield, it was always supposed that he simply followed the carriage, and had the wit to hide himself when we stopped on the road. He was terribly tired. He might well be thirsty!

I levied large contributions on the box of rusks which Aunt Maria had left by my bedside, for his benefit, and he supped well.

Then he curled himself up in his own proper place at my feet. He was intensely self-satisfied, and expressed his high idea of his own exploit by self-gratulatory "grumphs," as after describing many mystic circles, and scraping up the fair Marseilles quilt on some plan of his own, he brought his nose and tail together in a satisfactory position in his nest, and we passed our first night in London in dreamless and profound sleep.

# CHAPTER V

## MY COUSINS—MISS BLOMFIELD—
## THE BOY IN BLACK

My first letter to my father was the work of several days, and as my penmanship was not of a rapid order, it cost me a good deal of trouble. When it was finished it ran thus:

MY DEAR PAPA,

I hope you are quite well. i am quite well. Rubens is here and he is quite well. We dont no how he got here but i am verry glad. Ant Maria said well he cant be sent back now so he sleeps on my bed and i like London it is a kweer place the houses are very big and i like my cussens pretty well they are all gals their nozes are very big i like Polly.

Nurse is quite well so good-bye.

i am your very loving son,

REGINALD DACRE.

Though I cannot defend the spelling of the above document, I must say that it does not leave much to be added to the portrait of my cousins. But it will be more polite to introduce them separately, as they were presented to me.

I heard them, by the bye, before I saw them. It was whilst I was dressing, the morning after my arrival, that I heard sounds in the room below, which were interpreted by Nurse as being "Miss Maria doing her music." The peculiarity of Miss Maria's music was that after a scramble over the notes, suggestive of some one running to get impetus for a jump, and when the ear waited impatiently for the consummation, Miss Maria baulked her leap, so to speak, and got no farther, and began the scramble again, and stuck once more, and so on. And as, whilst finding the running passage quite too much for one hand, she struggled on with a different phrase in the other hand at the same time, instead of practising the two hands separately, her chances of final success seemed remote indeed. Then I heard the performance in peculiar circumstances. Nurse Bundle had opened my window, and about two minutes after my cousin commenced her practice, an organ-grinder in the street below began his. The subject of poor Maria's piece knew no completion, as she stuck halfway; but the organ-grinder's melodies only stopped for a touch to the mechanism, and Black-Eyed Susan passed into the Old Hundredth, awkwardly, but with hardly a perceptible pause. The effect of the joint performance was at first ludicrous, and by degrees maddening, especially when we had come to the Old Hundredth, which was so familiar in connection with the words of the Psalm.

"Three and four and—" began poor Maria afresh, with desperate resolution; and then off she went up the key-board; "one and two and three and four and, one and two and three and four and—"

"—joy—His—courts—un—to," ground the organ in the inevitable pause. And then my cousin took courage and made another start—"Three and four and one and two and," etc.; but at the old place the nasal notes of the other instrument evoked "al—ways," from my memory; and Maria pausing in despair, the Old Hundredth finished triumphantly, "For—it—is—seemly—so—to—do."

At half-past eight Maria stopped abruptly in the middle of her run, and Nurse took me down to the school-room for breakfast.

The school-room was high and narrow, with a very old carpet, and a very old piano, some books, two globes, and a good deal of feminine rubbish in the way of old work-baskets, unfinished sewing, etc. There were two long windows, the lower halves of which were covered with paint. This mattered the less as the only view from them was of backyards, roofs, and chimneys. Living as I did, so much alone with my father, I was at first oppressed by the number of petticoats in the room—five girls of ages ranging from twelve to six, and a grown-up lady in a spare brown stuff dress and spectacles.

As we entered she came quickly forward and shook Nurse by the hand.

"How do you do, Mrs. Bundle? Very glad to see you again, Mrs. Bundle."

Nurse Bundle shook hands first, and curtsied afterwards.

"I'm very well, thank you, ma'am, and hope you're the same. Master Reginald Dacre, ma'am. This lady is Miss Blomfield, Master Reginald; and I hope you'll behave properly, and give the lady no trouble."

"I'm the governess, my dear," said Miss Blomfield, emphatically. (She always "made a point" of announcing her dependent position to strangers. "It is best to avoid any awkwardness," she was wont to say; and I saw glances and smiles exchanged on this occasion between the girls.) Miss Blomfield was very kind to me. Indeed she was kind to every one. Her other peculiarities were conscientiousness and the fidgets, and tendencies to fine crochet, calomel, and Calvinism, and an abiding quality of harassing and being harassed, which I may here say is, I am convinced, a common and most unfortunate atmosphere of much of the process of education for girls of the upper and middle classes in England.

At this moment my aunt came in.

"Good morning, Miss Blomfield."

"Good morning, Mrs. Ascott," the governess hastily interposed. "I hope you're well this morning."

"Good morning, girls. Good morning, Nurse. How do you, Regie? All right this morning? Bless me, there's that dog! What an extraordinary affair it is! Mr. Ascott says he shall send it to the 'Gentleman's Magazine.' Well, he can't be sent back now, so I suppose he'll have to stop. And you must keep him out of mischief, Regie. Remember, he's not to come into the drawing-room. Mrs. Bundle, will you see to that? Miss Blomfield, will you kindly speak to Signor Rigi when he comes to-morrow—"

"Certainly, Mrs. Ascott," interposed the governess.

"—about that piece of Maria's? She doesn't seem to get on with it a bit."

"No, Mrs. Ascott."

"And I'm sure she's been practising it for a long time."

"Yes, Mrs. Ascott."

"Mr. Ascott says it makes his hand quite unsteady when he's shaving in the morning, to hear her always break off at one place."

The lines of harass on Miss Blomfield's countenance deepened visibly, and her crochet-needle trembled in her hand, whilst a despondent stolidity settled on Maria's face.

"Certainly, Mrs. Ascott. I'm very glad you've spoken. Thank you for mentioning it, Mrs. Ascott. It has distressed me very greatly, and been a great trouble on my mind for some time. I spoke very seriously to Maria last Sabbath on the subject" (symptoms of sniffling on poor Maria's part). "I believe she wishes to do her duty, and I may say I am anxious to do mine, in my position. Of course, Mrs. Ascott, I know you've a right to expect an improvement, and I shall be most happy to rise half an hour earlier, so as to give her a longer practice than the other young ladies, and only consider it my duty as your governess, Mrs. Ascott. I've felt it a great trouble, for I cannot imagine how it is that Maria does not improve in her music as Jane does, and I give them equal attention exactly; and what makes it more singular still is that Maria is very good at her sums—I have no fault to find whatever. But I regret to say it is not the case with Jane. I told her on Wednesday that I did not wish to make any complaint; but I feel it a duty, Mrs. Ascott, to let you know that her marks for arithmetic are not what you have a right to expect."

Here Miss Blomfield paused and wiped her eyes. Not that she was weeping, but over and above her short-sightedness she was troubled with a dimness of vision, which afflicted her more at some times than others. As she was in the habit of endeavouring to counteract the evils of a too constantly laborious and sedentary life, and of an anxious and desponding temperament, by large doses of calomel, her malady increased with painfully rapid strides. On this particular morning she had been busy since five o'clock, and neither she nor the girls (who rose at six) had had anything to eat, and they were all somewhat faint for want of a breakfast which was cooling on the table. Meanwhile a "humming in the head," to which *she* was subject, rendered Maria mercifully indifferent to the proposal to add an extra half-hour to her distasteful labours; and Miss Blomfield corrugated her eyebrows, and was conscientiously distressed and really puzzled that Mother Nature should give different gifts to her children, when their mother and teachers according to the flesh were so particular to afford them an equality of "advantages."

"Signor Rigi told me that Maria has not got so good an ear as Jane," said Mrs. Ascott. "However, perhaps it will be well to let Maria practise half an hour, and Jane do half an hour at her arithmetic on Saturday afternoons."

"Certainly, Mrs. Ascott."

"And now," said my aunt, "I must introduce the girls to Reginald. This is Maria, your eldest cousin, and nearly double your age, for she is twelve. This is Jane, two years younger. This is Helen; she is nine, and as tall as Jane, you see. This is Harriet, eight. And this is Mary—Polly, as papa calls her—and she is nineteen months younger than you, and a terrible tomboy already; so don't make her worse. This is your cousin, girls, Reginald Dacre. You must amuse him among you, and don't tease him, for he is not used to children."

We "shook hands" all round, and I liked Polly's hand the best. It was least froggy, cold, and spiritless.

Then Mrs. Ascott departed, and Maria (overpowered by the humming) "flopped" into her chair after a fashion that would certainly have drawn a rebuke from Miss Blomfield if an access of eye-dimness had not carried her to her own seat with little more grace.

Uncle Ascott had a large nose, and my cousins were the image of him and of each other. They were plain, lady-like, rather bouncing girls, with aquiline noses, voices with a family *twang* that was slightly nasal, long feet terribly given to chilblains, and long fingers, with which they all by turns practised the same exercises on the old piano on successive mornings before breakfast. When we became more intimate, I used to keep watch on the clock for the benefit of the one who was practising. At half-past eight she was released, and shutting up the book with a bang would scamper off, in summer to stretch herself, and in winter to warm her hands and toes. I used to watch their fingers with childish awe, wondering how such thin pieces of flesh and bone hit such hard blows to the notes without cracking, and being also somewhat puzzled by the run of good luck which seemed to direct their weak and random-looking skips and jumps to the keys at which they were aimed. I have seen them in tears over their "music," as it was called, but they were generally persevering, and in winter (so I afterwards discovered) invariably blue.

It was not till we had finished breakfast that Miss Blomfield became fairly conscious of the presence of Rubens, and when she did so her alarm was very great.

Considering what she suffered from her own proper and peculiar worries, it seemed melancholy to have to add to her burdens the hourly expectation of an outbreak of hydrophobia.

In vain I testified to the sweetness of Rubens' temper. It is undeniable that dogs do sometimes bite when you least expect it, and that some bites end in hydrophobia; and it was long before Miss Blomfield became reconciled to this new inmate of the school-room.

The girls, on the contrary, were delighted with my dog; and it was on this ground that we became friendly. My particular affection for Polly was also probably due to the discovery that with an incomparably stolid expression of countenance she was passing highly buttered pieces of bread under the table to Rubens at breakfast.

Polly was my chief companion. The other girls were good-natured, but they were constantly occupied in the school-room, and hours that were not nominally "lesson time" were given to preparing tasks for the next day. By a great and very unusual concession, Polly's lessons were shortened that she might bear me company. For the day or two before this was decided on I had been very lonely, and Cousin Polly's holiday brought much satisfaction both to me and to her; but it filled poor Miss Blomfield's mind with disquietude, scruples, and misgivings.

In the middle of the square where my uncle and aunt lived there was a garden, with trees, and grass, and gravel-walks; and here Polly and I played at hide and seek, and ran races, and chased each other and Rubens.

The garden was free to all dwellers in the square, and several other children besides ourselves were wont to play there. One day as I was strolling about, a little boy whom I had not seen before came down the walk and crossed the grass. He seemed to be a year or two older than myself, and caught my eye immediately by his remarkable beauty, and by the depth of the mourning which he wore. His features were exquisitely cut, and, in a child, one was not disposed to complain of their effeminacy. His long fair hair was combed—in royal fashion—down his back, a style at that time most unusual; his tightly-fitting jacket and breeches were black, bordered with deep crape; not even a white collar relieved his sombre attire, from which his fair face shone out doubly fair by contrast.

"Polly! Polly!" I cried, running to find my companion and guide, "who is that beautiful boy in black?"

"That's little Sir Lionel Damer," said Polly. "Good-morning, Leo!" and she nodded as he passed.

The boy just touched his hat, bent his head with a melancholy and yet half-comical dignity, and walked on.

"Who's he in mourning for?" I asked.

"His father and mother," said Polly. "They were drowned together, and now he is Sir Lionel."

I looked after him with sudden and intense sympathy. His mother and his father too! This indeed was sorrow deeper than mine. Surely his mother, like mine, must have been fair and beautiful, so much beauty and fairness had descended to him.

"Has he any sisters, Polly?" I asked.

Polly shook her head. "I don't think he has anybody," said she.

Then he also was an only son!

# CHAPTER VI

## THE LITTLE BARONET—DOLLS—CINDER PARCELS—THE OLD GENTLEMAN NEXT DOOR— THE ZOOLOGICAL GARDENS

The next time I saw Sir Lionel was about two days after-wards, in the afternoon, when the elder girls had gone for a drive in the carriage with Aunt Maria, and the others, with myself, were playing in the garden; Miss Blomfield being seated on a camp-stool reading a terrible article on "Rabies" in the Medical Dictionary.

Rubens and I had strolled away from the rest, and I was exercising him in some of his tricks when the little baronet passed us with his accustomed air of mingled melancholy, dignity, and self-consciousness. I was a good deal fascinated by him. Beauty has a strong attraction for children, and the depth of his weeds invested him with a melancholy interest, which has also great charms for the young. Then, to crown all, he mourned the loss of a young mother—and so did I. I involuntarily showed off Rubens as he approached, and he lingered and watched us. By a sort of impulse I took off my little hat, as I had been taught to do to strangers. He lifted his with a dismal grace and moved on.

But as he walked about I could see that he kept looking to

Juliana Horatia Ewing

where Rubens and I played upon the grass, and at last he came and sat down near us.

"Is that your dog?" he asked.

"Yes he's my dog," I answered.

"He seems very clever," said Sir Lionel. "Did you teach him all those tricks yourself?"

"Very nearly all," said I. "Rubens, shake hands with Sir Lionel."

"How do you know my name?" he asked.

"Polly told me," said I.

"Do you know Polly?" Sir Lionel inquired.

I stared, forgetting that of course he did not know who I was, and answered—

"She's my cousin."

"What's your name?" he asked.

I told him.

"Do you like Polly?" he continued.

"Very much," I said, warmly.

It was with a ludicrous imitation of some grown-up person's manner that he added, in perfect gravity—

"I hope you are not in love with her?"

"Oh, dear no!" I cried, hastily, for I had had enough of that joke with Miss Eliza Burton.

"Then that is all right," said the little baronet; "let us be friends." And friends we became. "Call me Leo, and I'll call you Reginald," said the little gentleman; and so it was.

I think it is not doing myself more than justice if I say that to this, my first friendship, I was faithful and devoted. Leo, for his part, was always affectionate, and he had an admiration for Rubens which went a long way with Rubens' master. But he was a little spoiled and capricious, and, like many people of rather small capacities (whether young or old), he was often unintentionally inconsiderate. In those days my affection waited willingly upon his; but I know now that in a quiet amiable way he was selfish. I was blessed myself with an easy temper, and at that time it had ample opportunities of accommodating itself to the whims of my friend Leo and my cousin Polly. Not that Polly was like Sir Lionel in any way whatever. But she was quick-tempered and resolute. She was much more clever for her age than I was for mine. She was very decided and rapid in her views and proceedings, very generous and affectionate also, and not at all selfish. But her qualities and those of Leo came to the same thing as far as I was concerned. I invariably yielded to them both.

Between themselves, I may say, they squabbled systematically, and were never either friends or enemies for two days together.

Polly and I never quarrelled. I did her behests manfully, as a general rule; and if her sway became intolerable, I complained and bewailed, on which she relented, being as easily moved to pity as to wrath.

As the weather grew more chill, we seldom went out except

in the morning. In the afternoon Polly and I (sometimes accompanied by Leo) played in the nursery at the top of the house.

Now and then the other girls would come up, and "play at dolls" with Polly. On these occasions the treatment I experienced was certainly hard. They were soon absorbed in dressing and undressing, sham meals, sham lessons. and all the domestic romance of doll-life, in which, according to my poor abilities, I should have been most happy to have taken a part. But, on the unwarrantable assumption that "boys could not play at dolls," the only part assigned me in the puppet comedy was to take the dolls' dirty clothes to and from an imaginary wash in a miniature wheelbarrow. I did for some time assume the character of dolls' medical man with considerable success; but having vaccinated the kid arm of one of my patients too deeply on a certain occasion with a big pin, she suffered so severely from loss of bran that I was voted a practitioner of the old school, and dismissed. I need hardly say that this harsh decision proved the ruin of my professional prospects, and I was sent back to my wheelbarrow. It was when we were tired of our ordinary amusements, during a week of wet weather, that Polly and I devised a new piece of fun to enliven the monotony of the hours when we were shut up in that town nursery at the top of the house.

Outside the nursery-windows were iron bars—a sensible precaution of Aunt Maria against accidents to "the little ones." One day when the window was slightly open, and Polly and I were hanging on the window-ledge, in attitudes that fully justified the precautionary measure of a grating, a bit of paper which was rolled up in Polly's hand escaped from her grasp, and floated down into the street. In a moment Polly and I were standing on the window-ledge, peering down—to the best of our ability—into the square and into the area depths below. Like a snow-flake in summer, we saw our paper-twist lying on the pavement; but our delight rose to ecstasy when a portly passer-by stooped and picked up the document and carefully examined it.

Out of this incident arose a systematic amusement, which, in advance of our age, we called "the parcel post."

By shoving aside the fire-guard in the absence of our nurses, we obtained some cinders, with which we repaired to our post at the window, thus illustrating that natural proclivity of children to places of danger which is the bane of parents and guardians. Here we fastened up little fragments of cinder in pieces of writing-paper, and having secured them tidily with string, we dropped these parcels through the iron bars as into a post-office. It was a breathless moment when they fell through space like shooting stars. It was a triumph if they cleared the area. But the aim and the end of our labours was to see one of our missives attract the notice of a passer-by, then excite his curiosity, and finally—if he opened it—rouse his unspeakable disgust and disappointment.

Like other tricksters, our game lasted long because of the ever-green credulity of our "public." In the ever-fresh stream of human life which daily flowed beneath our windows, there were sure to be one or more pedestrians who, with varying expressions of conscientious responsibility, unprincipled appropriation, or mere curiosity, would open our parcels, either to ascertain what trinket should be restored to its owner, or to keep what was to be got, or to see what there was to be seen.

One day when we dropped one of our parcels at the feet of a lady who was going by, she nonplussed us very effectually by ringing the bell and handing in to the footman "something which had been accidentally dropped from one of the upper windows." Fortunately for us the parcel did not reach Aunt Maria; Polly intercepted it.

As the passers-by never wearied of our parcels, I do not know when we should have got tired of our share of the fun, but for an occurrence which brought the amusement suddenly to an end. One afternoon we had made up the neatest of little white-paper parcels, worthy of having come from a jeweller's, and I clambered on to the window-seat that I might drop it successfully (and quite clear of the area) into the street. Just as I dropped it, there passed an elderly gentleman very precisely dressed, with a gold-headed cane, and a very well-brushed hat. Pop! I let the cinder parcel fall on to his beaver, from which it rebounded to his feet. The old gentleman looked quickly up, our eyes met, and I felt convinced that he saw that I had thrown it. I called Polly, and as she reached my side the old gentleman untied and examined the parcel. When he came to the cinder, he looked up once more, and Polly jumped from the window with a prolonged "Oh!"

"What's the matter?" I asked.

"Oh, dear!" cried Polly; "it's the old gentleman next door!"

For several days we lived in unenviable suspense. Every morning did we expect to be summoned from the school-room to be scolded by Aunt Maria. Every afternoon we dreaded the arrival of "the old gentleman next door" to make his formal complaint, and, whenever the front-door bell rang, Polly and I literally "shook in our shoes."

But several days passed, and we heard nothing of it. We had given up the practice in our fright, but had some thoughts of beginning again, as no harm had come to us.

One evening (by an odd coincidence, my birthday was on the morrow) as Polly and I were putting away our playthings preparatory to being dressed to go down to dessert, a large brown-paper parcel was brought into the nursery addressed jointly to me and my cousin.

"It's a birthday present for you, Regie!" Polly cried.

"But there's your name on it, Polly," said I.

"It must be a mistake," said Polly. But she looked very much pleased, nevertheless; and so, I have no doubt, did I. We cut the string, we tore off the first thick covering. The present, whatever it might be, was securely wrapped a second time in finer brown paper and carefully tied.

"It's *very* carefully done up," said I, cutting the second string.

"It must be something nice," said Polly, decisively; "that's why it's taken such care of."

If Polly's reasoning were just, it must have been something very nice indeed, for under the second wrapper was a third, and under the third was a fourth, and under the fourth was a fifth, and under the fifth was a sixth, and under the sixth was a seventh. We were just on the point of giving it up in despair when we came to a box. With some difficulty we got the lid open, and took out one or two folds of paper. Then there was a lot of soft shavings, such as brittle toys and gimcracks are often packed in, and among the shavings was—a small neatly-folded white-paper parcel. *And inside the parcel was a cinder.*

We certainly looked very foolish as we stood before our present. I do not think any of the people we had taken in had looked so thoroughly and completely so. We were both on the eve of crying, and both ended by laughing. Then Polly—in those trenchant tones which recalled Aunt Maria forcibly to one's mind—said,

"Well! we quite deserve it."

The "parcel-post" was discontinued.

We had no doubt as to who had played us this trick. It was the old gentleman next door. He was a wealthy, benevolent, and rather eccentric old bachelor. It was his custom to take an early walk for the good of his health in the garden of the square, and he sometimes took an evening stroll in the same place for pleasure. Somehow or other he had made a speaking acquaintance with Miss Blomfield, and we afterwards discovered that he had made all needful inquiries as to the names, etc., of Polly and myself from her—she, however, being quite innocent as to the drift of his questions.

I should certainly not have selected the old gentleman's hat to drop our best parcel on to, if I had known who he was. I was not likely to forget his face now.

I soon got to know all our neighbours by sight. On one side of us was the old gentleman, whose name was Bartram; on the other side lived Sir Lionel Damer. He was staying with his guardian, an old Colonel Sinclair; and when my father came up to town he and this Colonel Sinclair discovered that they were old school-fellows, which Leo and I looked upon as a good omen for our friendship.

Polly and I and Nurse Bundle became as learned in gossip as any one else who lives in a town, and is constantly looking out of the window. We knew the (bird's-eye) appearance of everybody on our side of the square, their servants, their cats and dogs, their carriages, and even their tradesmen. If one of the neighbours changed his milkman, or there came so much as a new muffin man to the square, we were all agog. One day I saw Polly upon our perch, struggling to get her face close to the glass, and much hindered by the size of her nose. I felt sure that there was *something* down below—at least a new butcher's boy. So I was not surprised when she called me to "come and look."

"Who is it?" said Polly.

"I don't know," said I.

And then we both stared on, as if by downright hard looking we could discover the name of the gentleman who had just come down the steps from Colonel Sinclair's house. He was a short slight man, young, and with sandy hair. Neither of us had seen him before. Having the good fortune to see him return to Colonel Sinclair's house, about two hours later, I hurried with the news to Polly; and we resolved to get to see Leo as soon as possible, and satisfy our curiosity respecting the stranger. So in the afternoon we sent a message to invite him to come and play with us in the square, but we received the answer that "Sir Lionel was engaged."

Later on he came into the square, and the stranger with him. Polly and I and Rubens were together on a seat; but when Leo saw us he gave a scanty nod and went off in the opposite direction, leaning on the arm of the stranger and apparently absorbed in talking to him. I was rather hurt by his neglect of us. But Polly said positively,

"That is Leo's way. He likes new friends. But when he treats me like that, I do not speak to him for a week afterwards."

That evening a cab carried off the stranger, and next day Leo came to us in the square, all smiles and friendliness.

"I've been so wanting to see you!" he cried, in the most devoted tones. But Polly only took up her doll, and with her impressive nose in the air, walked off to the house.

I could not quarrel with Leo myself, and we were soon as friendly as ever.

"I want to tell you some news, Regie," he said. "Colonel Sinclair has decided that I am to have a tutor."

"Are you glad?" I asked.

"Yes, very," said Sir Lionel. "You see I like him very much—I mean the tutor. He was here yesterday. You saw him with me. He is going to be a clergyman. He has been at Cambridge, and he plays the flute."

For a long time Leo enlarged to me upon the merits of his tutor that was to be; and when I went back to Polly the news I had to impart served to atone for my not having joined her in snubbing the capricious Sir Lionel. As for him, he was very restless under Polly's displeasure, and finally apologized, on which Polly gave him a sound scolding, which, to my surprise, he took in the utmost good part, and we were all once more the best possible friends.

That visit to London was an era in my life. It certainly was most enjoyable, and it did me a world of good, body and mind. When my father came up, we enjoyed it still more. He coaxed holidays for the girls even out of Aunt Maria, and took us (Leo and all) to places of amusement. With him we went to the Zoological Gardens. The monkeys attracted me indescribably, and I seriously proposed to my father to adopt one or two of them as brothers for me. I felt convinced that if they were properly dressed and taught they would be quite companionable, and I said so, to my father's great amusement, and to the scandal of Nurse Bundle, who was with us.

"I fear you would never teach them to talk, Regie," said my father; "and a friend who could neither speak to you nor understand you when you spoke to him would be a very poor companion, even if he could dance on the top of a barrel-organ and crack hard nuts."

"But, papa, babies can't talk at first," said I; "they have to be taught."

Now by good luck for my argument there stood near us a country woman with a child in her arms to whom she was holding out a biscuit, repeating as she did so, "Ta!" in that expectant tone which is supposed to encourage childish efforts to pronounce the abbreviated form of thanks.

"Now look, papa!" I cried, "that's the way I should teach a monkey. If I were to hold out a bit of cake to him, and say, 'Ta,'"—(and as I spoke I did so to a highly intelligent little gentleman who sat close to the bars of the cage with his eyes on my face, as if he were well aware that a question of deep importance to himself was being discussed)—

"He would probably snatch it out of your hand without further ceremony," said my father. And, dashing his skinny fingers through the bars, this was, I regret to say, precisely what the little gentleman did. I was quite taken aback; but as we turned round, to my infinite delight, the undutiful baby snatched the biscuit from its mother's hand after a fashion so remarkably similar that we all burst out laughing, and I shouted in triumph,

"Now, papa! children do it too."

"Well, Regie," he answered, "I think you have made out a good case. But the question which now remains is, whether Mrs. Bundle will have your young friends in the nursery."

But Mrs. Bundle's horror at my remarks was too great to admit of her even entering into the joke.

The monkeys were somewhat driven from my mind by the wit and wisdom of the elephant, and the condescension displayed by so large an animal in accepting the light refreshment of penny buns. After he had had several, Leo began to tease him, holding out a bun and snatching it away again. As he was holding it out for the fourth or fifth time, the elephant extended his trunk as usual, but instead of directing it towards the bun, he deliberately snatched the black velvet cap from Leo's head and swallowed it with a grunt of displeasure. Leo was first frightened, and then a good deal annoyed by the universal roar of laughter which his misfortune occasioned. But he was a good-tempered boy, and soon joined in the laugh himself. Then, as we could not buy him a new cap in the Gardens, he was obliged to walk about for the rest of the time bare-headed; and many were the people who turned round to look a second time after the beautiful boy with the long fair hair—a fact of which Master Lionel was not quite unconscious, I think.

My aunt kindly pressed us to remain with her over Christmas. I longed to see the pantomime, having heard much from my cousins and from Leo of its delights—and of the harlequin, columbine, and clown. But my father wanted to be at home again, and he took me and Rubens and Nurse Bundle with him at the end of November.

# CHAPTER VII

## POLLY AND I RESOLVE TO BE "VERY RELIGIOUS"—DR. PEPJOHN—THE ALMS-BOX—THE BLIND BEGGAR

I must not forget to speak of an incident which had a considerable influence on my character at this time. The church which my uncle and his family "attended," as it was called, was one of those most dreary places of worship too common at that time, in London and elsewhere. It was ugly outside, but the outside ugliness was as nothing compared with the ugliness within. The windows were long and bluntly rounded at the top, and the sunlight was modified by scanty calico blinds, which, being yellow with age and smoke, *toned* the light in rather an agreeable manner. Mouldings of a pattern one sees about common fireplaces ran everywhere with praiseworthy impartiality. But the great principle of the ornamental work throughout was a principle only too prevalent at the date when this particular church was last "done up." It was imitations of things not really there, and which would have been quite out of place if they had been there. For instance, pillars and looped-up curtains painted on flat walls, with pretentious shadows, having no reference to the real direction of the light. At the east end some Hebrew letters, executed as journeymen painters usually do execute them, had a less cheerful look than the highly-coloured lion

Juliana Horatia Ewing

and unicorn on the gallery in front. The clerk's box, the reading-desk, and the pulpit, piled one above another, had a symmetrical effect, to which the umbrella-shaped sounding-board above gave a distant resemblance to a Chinese pagoda. The only things which gave warmth or colour to the interior as a whole were the cushions and pew curtains. There were plenty of them, and they were mostly red. These same curtains added to the sense of isolation, which was already sufficiently attained by the height of the pew walls and their doors and bolts. I think it was this—and the fact that, as the congregation took no outward part in the prayers except that of listening to them, Polly and I had nothing to do—and we could not even hear the old gentleman who usually "read prayers"—which led us into the very reprehensible habit of "playing at houses" in Uncle Ascott's gorgeously furnished pew. Not that we left our too tightly stuffed seats for one moment, but as we sat or stood, unable to see anything beyond the bombazine curtains (which, intervening between us and the distant parson, made our hearing what he said next to impossible), we amused ourselves by mentally "pretending" a good deal of domestic drama, in which the pew represented a house; and we related our respective "plays" to each other afterwards when we went home.

Wrong as it was, we did not intend to be irreverent, though I had the grace to feel slightly shocked when after a cheerfully lighted evening service, at which the claims of a missionary society had been enforced, Polly confided to me, with some triumph in her tone, "I pretended a theatre, and when the man was going round with the box upstairs, I pretended it was oranges in the gallery."

I had more than once felt uneasy at our proceedings, and I now told Polly that I thought it was not right, and that we ought to "try to attend." I rather expected her to resent my advice, but she said that she had "sometimes thought it was wrong" herself; and we resolved to behave better for the future, and indeed really did give up our unseasonable game.

Few religious experiences fill one with more shame and self-reproach than the large results from very small efforts in the right direction. Polly and I prospered in our efforts to "attend." I may say for myself that, child as I was, I began to find a satisfaction and pleasure in going to church, though the place was hideous, the ritual dreary, and the minister mumbling. When by chance there was a nice hymn, such as, "Glory to Thee," or "O GOD, our help in ages past," we were quite happy. We also tried manfully to "attend" to the sermons, which, considering the length and abstruseness of them, was, I think, creditable to us. I fear we felt it to be so, and that about this time we began to be proud of the texts we knew, and of our punctilious propriety in the family pew, and of the resolve which we had taken in accordance with my proposal to Polly—

"Let us be very religious."

One Saturday Miss Blomfield was a good deal excited about a certain clergyman who was to preach in our church next Sunday, and as the services were now a matter of interest to us, Polly and I were excited too. I had been troubled with toothache all the week, but this was now better, and I was quite able to go to church with the rest of the family.

The general drift of the sermon, even its text, have long since faded from my mind; but I do remember that it contained so highly coloured a peroration on the Day of Judgment and the terrors of Hell, that my horror and distress knew no bounds; and when the sermon was ended, and we began to sing, "From lowest depths of woe," I burst into a passion of weeping. The remarkable part of the incident was that, the rest of the party having sat with their noses in the air quite undistressed by the terrible eloquence of the preacher, Aunt Maria never for a moment guessed at the real cause of my tears. But as soon as we were all in the carriage (it was a rainy evening, and we had driven to church), she said—

"That poor child will never have a minute's peace while that tooth's in his head. Thomas! Drive to Dr. Pepjohn's."

Polly did say, "Is it very bad, Regie?" But Aunt Maria answered for me—"Can't you see it's bad, child? Leave him alone."

I was ashamed to confess the real cause of my outburst, and suffered for my disingenuousness in Dr. Pepjohn's consulting-room.

"Show Dr. Pepjohn which it is, Regie," said my aunt; and, with tears that had now become simply hysterical, I pointed to the tooth that had ached.

"Just allow me to touch it," said Dr. Pepjohn, inserting his fat finger and thumb into my mouth. "I won't hurt you, my little man," he added, with the affable mendaciousness of his craft. Fortunately for me it was rather loose, and a couple of hard wrenches from the doctor's expert fingers brought it out.

"You think me very cruel, now, don't you, my little man?" said the jocose gentleman, as we were taking leave.

"I don't think you're cruel," I answered, candidly; "but I think you tell fibs, for it *did* hurt."

The doctor laughed long and loudly, and said I was quite an original, which puzzled me extremely. Then he gave me sixpence, with which I was much pleased, and we parted good friends.

My father was with us on the following Sunday, and he did not go to the church Aunt Maria went to. I went to the one to which he went. This church was very well built and appropriately decorated. The music was good, the responses of the congregation hearty, and the service altogether was much better adapted to awaken and sustain the interest of a child than those I had hitherto been to in London.

"You know we *couldn't* play houses in the church where Papa goes," I told Polly on my return, and I was very anxious that she should go with us to the evening service. She did go, but I am bound to confess that she decided on a loyal preference for the service to which she had been accustomed, and, like sensible people, we agreed to differ in our tastes.

"There's no clerk at your church, you know," said Polly, to whom a gap in the threefold ministry of clerk, reader, and preacher, symbolized by the "three-decker" pulpit, was ill atoned for by the chanting of the choir.

In quite a different way, I was as much impressed by the sermons at the new church as I had been by that which cost me a tooth.

One sermon especially upon the duties of visiting the sick and imprisoned, feeding the hungry, and clothing the naked, made an impression on me that years did not efface. I made the most earnest resolutions to be active in deeds of kindness "when I was a man," and, not being troubled by consi-derations of political economy, I began my charitable career by dividing what pocket money I had in hand amongst the street-sweepers and mendicants nearest to our square.

I soon converted Polly to my way of thinking; and we put up a money-box in the nursery, in imitation of the alms-box in church. I am ashamed to confess that I was guilty of the meanness of changing a sixpence which I had dedicated to our "charity-box" into twelve half-pence, that I might have the satisfaction of making a dozen distinct contributions to the fund.

But, despite all its follies, vanities, and imperfections (and what human efforts for good are not stained with folly, vanity, and imperfection?), our benevolence was not without sincerity or self-denial, and brought its own invariable reward of increased willingness to do more; according to the deep wisdom of the poet—

"In doing is this knowledge won:
To see what yet remains undone."

We really did forego many a toy and treat to add to our charitable store; and I began then a habit of taxing what money I possessed, by taking off a fixed proportion for "charity," which I have never discontinued, and to the advantages of which I can most heartily testify. When a self-indulgent civilization goads all classes to live beyond their incomes, and tempts them not to include the duty of almsgiving in the expenditure of those incomes, it is well to remove a due proportion of what one has beyond the reach of the ever-growing monster of extravagance; and, being decided upon in an unbiased and calm moment, it is the less likely to be too much for one's domestic claims, or too little for one's religious duty. It frees one for ever from that grudging and often comical spasm of meanness which attacks so many even wealthy people when they are asked to give, because, among all the large "expenses" to which their goods are willingly made liable, the expense of giving alms of those goods has never been fairly counted as an item not less needful, not less imperative, not less to be felt as a deduction from the remainder, not less life-long and daily, than the expenses of rent, and dress, and dinner-parties.

We had, as I say, no knowledge of political economy, and it must be confessed that the objects of our charity were on more than one occasion most unworthy.

"Oh, Regie, dear," Polly cried one day, rushing up to me as she returned from a walk (I had a cold, and was in the nursery), "there is such a poor, poor man at the corner of— Street. I do think we ought to give him all that's left in the box. He's quite blind, and he reads out of a book with such queer letters. It's one of the Gospels, he says; so he must be very good, for he reads it all day long. And he can't have any home, for he sits in the street. And he's got a ticket on his back to say 'Blind,' and 'Taught at the Blind School.' And as I passed he was reading quite loud. And I heard him say, 'Now Barabbas was a robber.' Oh, he *is* such a poor man! And you know, Regie, he *must* be good, for *we* don't sit reading our Bibles all day long."

I at once gave my consent to the box being emptied in favour of this very poor and very pious man; and at the first opportunity Polly took the money to her *protege*.

"He was so much pleased!" she reported on her return. "He seemed quite surprised to get so much. And he said, 'GOD bless you, miss!' I wish you'd been there, Regie. I said, 'It's not all from me.' He *was* so much pleased!"

"How did he know you were a *miss*, I wonder?" said I.

"I suppose it was my voice," said Polly, after a pause.

As soon as I could go out, I went to see the blind man. As I drew near, he was—as Polly told me—reading aloud. The regularity and rapidity with which his fingers ran over line after line, as if he were rubbing out something on a slate, were most striking; and as I stood beside him I distinctly heard him read the verse, "Now Barabbas was a robber." It was a startling coincidence to find him still reading the words which Polly overheard, especially as they were not in any way remarkably adapted for the subject of a prolonged meditation.

Much living alone with grown-up people had, I think, helped towards my acquiring a habit I had of "brown studying," turning things over, brewing them, so to speak, in my mind. I stood pondering the peculiarities of the object of our charity for some moments, during which he was elaborately occupied in turning over a leaf of his book. Presently I said—

"What makes you say it out loud when you read?"

He turned his head towards me, blinking and rolling his eyes, and replied in impressive tones—

"It's the pleasure I takes in it, sir."

Now as he blinked I watched his eyes with mingled terror, pity, and curiosity. At this moment a stout and charitable-looking old gentleman was passing, between whom and my blind friend I was standing. And as he passed he threw the blind man some coppers. But in the moment before he did so, and when there seemed a possibility of his passing without what I suspect was a customary dole, such a sharp expression came into the scarcely visible pupils of the blind man's half-shut eyes that (never suspecting that his blindness was feigned, but for the moment convinced that he had seen the old gentleman) I exclaimed, without thinking of the absurdity of my inquiry—

"Was it at the Blind School you learnt to see so well with your blind eyes?"

The "very poor man" gave me a most unpleasant glance out of his "sightless orbs," and taking up his stool, and muttering something about its being time to go home, he departed.

Some time afterwards I learnt what led me to believe that he had the best possible reason for being able to "see so well with his blind eyes." He was not blind at all.

# CHAPTER VIII

## VISITING THE SICK

I had been quite prepared to find Polly a willing convert to my charitable schemes, but I had not expected to find in Cousin Helen so strong an ally as she proved. But our ideas were no novelty to her, as we soon discovered. In truth, at nine years old, she was a bit of an enthusiast. She read with avidity religious biographies furnished by Miss Blomfield. She was delicate in health, but reticent and resolute in character. She was ready for any amount of self-sacrifice. She contributed liberally to our box; and I fancy that she and Polly continued it after I had gone back to Dacrefield.

My new ideas were not laid aside on my return home. To the best of my ability I had given Nurse Bundle an epitome of the sermon on alms—deeds which had so taken my fancy, and I have reason to believe that she was very proud of my precocious benevolence. Whilst the subject was under discussion betwixt us, she related many anecdotes of the good deeds of the "young gentlemen and ladies" in a certain clergyman's family where she had lived as nursemaid in her younger days; and my imagination was fired by dreams of soup-cans, coal-clubs, linsey petticoats comforting the rheumatic limbs of aged women, opportune blankets in winter, Sunday-school classes, etc., etc.

"My dear!" said Nurse Bundle, almost with tears in her eyes, "you're for all the world your dear mamma over again. Keep them notions, my dear, when you're a grown gentleman, and there'll be a blessing on all you do. For in all reason it's you that'll have to look to your pa's property and tenants some time."

My father, though not himself an adept in the details of what is commonly called "parish work," was both liberal and kind-hearted. He liked my knowing the names of his tenants, and taking an interest in their families. He was well pleased to respond by substantial help when Nurse Bundle and I pleaded for this sick woman or that unshod child, as my mother had pleaded in old days. As for Nurse Bundle, she had a code of virtues for "young ladies and gentlemen," as such, and charity to the poor was among them. Though I confess that I think she regarded it more in the light of a grace adorning a certain station, than as a duty incumbent upon all men.

So I came to know most of the villagers; and being a quaint child, with a lively and amusing curiosity, which some little refinement and good-breeding stayed from degenerating into impertinence, I was, I believe, very popular.

One afternoon, during the spring that followed our return from London, I had strolled out with Rubens, and was bowling my hoop towards one of the lodges when a poor woman passed by on the drive (which was a public road through the park), her apron to her face, weeping bitterly. I stopped her, and asked what was the matter, and finally made out that she had been to some sale at a farmhouse near, where a certain large blanket had "gone for" five shillings. That she had scraped five shillings together, and had intended to bid for it, but had (with eminent stupidity) managed just to be out of the way when the blanket was sold; and that it had gone for the very sum she could have afforded, to another woman who would only part with it for six and sixpence—eighteenpence more than the price she had paid for it.

The poor woman wept, and said she had had hard work to "raise" the five shillings, and could not possibly find one and sixpence more. And yet she did want the blanket badly, for she had a boy sick in bed, and his throat was so bad—he suffered a deal from the cold, and there wasn't a decent "rag of a blanket" in her house. I did not quite follow her long story, but I gathered that one and sixpence would put an end to her troubles, and at once offered to fetch her the money.

"Where do you live?" I asked.

"The white cottage just beyond the gate, love," she answered.

"I will bring you the money," said I. For to say the truth, I was rather pompous and important about my charitable deeds, and did not dislike playing the part of Sir Bountiful in the cottages. In this case, too, it was a kindness not to take the woman back to the hall, for she had left the sick child alone; and when I arrived at the cottage with the money he complained bitterly at the idea of her leaving him again to get the blanket.

"Let me go a minute, love, and I'll fetch Mrs. Taylor to sit with thee till I get the blanket."

"I don't want a blanket," fretted the child; "I be too hot as 'tis. I don't want to be 'lone."

"If you'll only be a minute, I'll stop with him," said I; and there was some kindness in the offer, for I was really afraid of the boy with his heavy angry eyes and fever petulance.

The woman gladly accepted it, and hurried off, despite the child's fretful tears, and his refusing to see in "the young gentleman's" condescension the honour which his mother pointed out. No doubt she only meant to be "a minute," and Mrs. Taylor's dwelling was, to my knowledge, near; but I suppose she had to tell, and her friends to hear, the whole history of the sale, her disappointment and subsequent relief, as a preliminary measure. After which it is probable that Mrs. Taylor had to look at her pie in the oven, or attend to some similar and pressing domestic duty before she could leave her house; and so it was nearly half an hour before they came to my relief. And all this time the sick boy tossed and moaned, and cried for water. I gave him some from a mug on the table, not so much from any precocious gift for sick nursing (for I was simply "frightened out of my wits"), but because the imperative tone of his demand forced me involuntarily into doing what he wanted. He grumbled, when between us we spilt the water on his clothes, and then, soothed for a few seconds, he lay down, till the fever, like a possessing demon, tossed him about once more, and his throat became as parched as ever, and again he moaned for "a drink," and we repeated the process. This time the mug was emptied, and when he called a third time I could only say, "The mug's empty."

"There's a pot behind the door," he muttered, impatiently; "look sharp!"

Now food, and drink, and all other necessaries of life came to me without effort or seeking, and I was as little accustomed as any other rich man's son to forage for supplies; but on this occasion circumstances forced out of me a helpfulness which necessity early teaches to the poor. I became dimly cognizant of the fact that water does not spring spontaneously in carafes, nor take a delicate colour and flavour in toast-and-water jugs of itself. I found the water-pot, replenished the mug, and went back to my patient. By the time his mother returned I had become quite clever in checking the spasmodic clutches which spilt the cold water into his neck.

From what Mrs. Taylor said to her friend, it was evident that she disapproved in some way of my presence, and the boy's mother replied to her whispered remonstrances, "I was *that* put out, I never thought;" which I have no doubt was strictly true.

As I afterwards learnt, she got the blanket, and never ceased to laud my generosity.

I was rather proud of it myself, and it was not without complacency that I recounted to Nurse Bundle my first essay in "visiting the sick."

But complacency was the last feeling my narrative awoke in Mrs. Bundle. She was alarmed out of all presence of mind; and her indignation with the woman who had requited my kindness by allowing me to go into a house infected with fever knew no bounds. She had no pity to spare for her when the news reached us that the child was dead.

Nothing further came of it for some time. Days passed, and it was almost forgotten, only I became decidedly ill-tempered. A captious irritability possessed me, alternating with fits of unaccountable fatigue. At that time I was always either tired or cross, and sometimes both. I must have made Nurse Bundle very uncomfortable. I was so little happy, for my own share, that when after a day's headache I was put to bed as an invalid, it was a delicious relief to be acknowledged to be ill, to throw off clothes and occupation, and shut my eyes and be nursed.

This happiness lasted for about half an hour. Then I began to shiver, and, through no lack of blankets my teeth were soon chattering and the bed shaking under me, as it had been with the village boy. But when this was succeeded by burning heat, and intolerable, consuming restlessness, I would have been glad to shiver again. And then my mind wandered with a restlessness more intolerable than the tossing of my body; and all boundaries of time, and place, and person became confused and indefinitely extended, and hot hours were like ages, and I thought I was that other boy, and that myself would not wait upon him; and the only sensible words I spoke were cries for drink; and so the fever got me fairly into its clutches.

Juliana Horatia Ewing

# CHAPTER IX

## "PEACE BE TO THIS HOUSE"

I can appreciate now what my father and Nurse Bundle must have suffered during my dangerous illness. It was not a common tie that bound my father's affections to my life. Not only was I his son, I was his only son. Moreover, I was the only living child of the beloved wife of his youth—all that remained to him of my fair mother. Then I was the heir to his property, the hope of his family, and, without undue egotism, I may say, from what I have been told, that I was a quaint, original, and (thanks to Mrs. Bundle) not ill-behaved child, and that, for a while at least, I should have been much missed in the daily life of the household.

Mrs. Cadman told me, long afterwards, exactly how many days and nights Nurse Bundle passed in my sick chamber, "and never had her clothes off;" and if the wearing of clothes had been one of the sharpest torments of the Inquisition, Mrs. Cadman could not have spoken in a hollower tone, or thrown more gloom round the announcement.

That, humanly speaking, my good and loving nurse saved my life, I must ever remember with deep gratitude. There are stages of fever, when, as they say, "a nurse is everything;" and a very little laziness, selfishness, or inattention on Nurse

Bundle's part would probably have been my death-warrant. But night and day she never relaxed her vigilance for one instant of the crisis of my malady. She took nothing for granted, would trust no one else, but herself saw every order of the doctor carried out, and, at a certain stage, fed me every ten minutes, against my will, coaxing me to obedience, and never losing heart or temper for one instant. And this although my petulance and not infrequent assurances that I wished and preferred to die—"I was so tired"—within the sick room, and my father's despair and bitter groan that he would sacrifice every earthly possession to keep me alive, outside it, would have caused many people to lose their heads. In such an hour many a foolish, gossiping, half-educated woman, by absolute faithfulness to the small details of her trust, by the complete laying aside of personal needs and personal feelings, rises to the sublimity of duty, and, ministering to the wants of another with an unselfish vigilance almost perfect, earns that meed of praise from men, which from time to time persists, in grateful hyperbole, to liken her sex to the angels.

My poor father, whose irrepressible distress led to his being forbidden to enter my room, powerless to help, and therefore without alleviation for his anxiety, simply hung upon Nurse Bundle's orders and reports, and relied utterly on her. Fortunately for his own health, she gained sufficient influence to insist, almost as peremptorily as in my case, upon his taking food. Often afterwards did she describe how he and Rubens sat outside the door they were not allowed to enter; and she used to declare that when she came out, Rubens, as well as my father, turned an anxious and expectant countenance towards her, and that both alike seemed to await and to understand her report of my condition.

Only once did Nurse Bundle's self-possession threaten to fail her. It was on my repeated and urgent request to "have the clergyman to pray with me."

Mrs. Bundle, like most uneducated people, rather regarded the visitation of the sick by the parish clergyman as a sort of extreme unction or last sacrament. And to send for the parson seemed to her tantamount to dismissing the doctor and ringing the passing bell. My father was equally averse from the idea on other grounds. Moreover, our old rector had gone, and the lately-appointed one was a stranger, and rather an eccentric stranger, by all accounts.

For my own part, I had a strong interest in the new rector. His Christian name was the same as my own, which I felt to constitute a sort of connection; and the tales I had heard in the village of his peculiarities had woven a sort of ecclesiastical romance about him in my mind. He had come from some out-of-the-way parish in the west of England, where his people, being thoroughly used to his ways, took them as a matter of course. It was his scrupulous custom to conform as minutely as possible to the canons of the Church, as well as to the rubrics of the Prayer Book, and this to the point of wearing shoes instead of boots. He was a learned man, a naturalist, and an antiquarian. His appearance was remarkable, his hair being prematurely white, and yet thick, his eyes grey and expressive, with thick dark eyebrows, which actually met above them. For the rest, he was tall, thin, and dressed in obedience to the canons. I had been much interested in all that I had heard of him, and since my illness I had often thought of the unqualified note of praise I had heard sounded in his favour by more than one village matron, "He's beautiful in a sick-room." It was on one occasion when I heard this that I also heard that he was accustomed on entering the house to pronounce the appointed salutation, in the words of the Prayer Book, "Peace be to this house, and to all that dwell in it." And so it came about that, when my importunity and anxiety on the subject had overcome the scruples of my father and nurse, and they had decided to let me have my way rather than increase my malady by fretting, the new rector came into my room, and my first eager question was, "Did you say that—about Peace, you know—when you came in?"

"I did," said the rector; and as he spoke one of his merits became obvious. He had a most pleasing voice.

"Say it again!" I cried, petulantly.

"Peace be to this house, and to all that dwell in it," he repeated slowly, and with slightly upraised hand.

"That's Rubens and all," was my comment.

As I wished, the rector prayed by my bedside; and I think he must have been rather astonished by the fact that at points which struck me I rather groaned than said, "Amen." The truth is, I had once happened to go into a cottage where our old rector was praying by the bed of a sick old man—a Methodist—who groaned "Amen" at certain points in a manner which greatly impressed me, and I now did likewise, in that imitativeness of childhood which had helped to lead me to the fancy for surrounding my own sick bed with all the circumstances I had seen and heard of in such cases in the village. For this reason I had (to her hardly concealed distress) given Nurse Bundle, from time to time, directions as to my wishes in the event of my death. I remember especially, that I begged she would not fail to cover up all the furniture with white cloths, and to allow all my friends to come and see me in my coffin. Thus also I groaned and said "Amen"—"like a poor person"—at what I deemed suitable points, as the rector prayed.

He was not less wise in a sick room than Mrs. Bundle

Juliana Horatia Ewing

herself. He contrived to quieten instead of exciting me, and to the sound of his melodious voice reading in soothing monotone from my favourite book of the Bible—the Revelation of St. John the Divine—I finally fell asleep.

When the inspired description of the New Jerusalem ended, and my own dream began, I never knew. As I dreamed, it seemed a wonderful and beautiful vision, though all that I could ever remember of it in waking hours was the sheerest nonsense.

And this was the beginning of my acquaintance with the Rev. Reginald Andrewes.

# CHAPTER X

## CONVALESCENCE—MATRIMONIAL INTENTIONS—THE JOURNEY TO OAKFORD— OUR WELCOME

On the day when I first left my sick room, and was moved to a sofa in what had been my poor mother's boudoir, my father put fifty pounds into Nurse Bundle's hand, and sent another fifty to Mr. Andrewes for some communion vessels for the church, on which the rector had set his heart. They were both thank-offerings.

"I owe my son's recovery to GOD, and to you, Mrs. Bundle," said my father, with a certain elaborateness of speech to which he was given on important occasions. "No money could purchase such care as you bestowed on him, and no money can reward it; but it will be doing me a farther favour to allow me to think that, should sickness ever overtake yourself when we are no longer together, this little sum, laid by, may come in useful, and afford you a few comforts."

That first evening of my convalescence we were quite jubilant; but afterwards there were many weary days of weakness, irritability, and *ennui* on my part, and anxiety and disappointment on my father's. Rubens was a great comfort at this period. For his winning ways formed an interest, and

Juliana Horatia Ewing

served a little to vary the monotony of the hours when I was too weak to bear any definite amusement or occupation. It must have been about this time that a long cogitation with myself led to the following conversations with Nurse Bundle and my father:—

"How old are you, Nurse?" I inquired, one forenoon, when she had neatly arranged the tray containing my chop, wine, etc., by my chair.

"Five-and-fifty, love, come September," said Nurse Bundle.

"Do people ever marry when they are five-and-fifty, papa?" I asked that evening, as I lay languid and weary on the sofa.

"Yes, my dear boy, sometimes. But why do you want to know?"

"I think I shall marry Nurse Bundle when I am old enough," I said, with almost melancholy gravity. "She's a good deal older than I am; but I love her very much. And she would make me very comfortable. She knows my ways."

My father has often told me that he would have laughed aloud, but for the sad air of utter weariness over my helpless figure, the painful, unchildlike anxiousness on my thin face, and in my old-fashioned air and attitude. I have myself quite forgotten the occurrence.

At last this most trying time was over, but the fever had left me taller, weaker, and much in need of what doctors call "tone." All concerned in the care of me were now unanimous in declaring that I must have a "change of air."

There was some little difficulty in deciding where to go. Another visit to Aunt Maria was out of the question. Even if

London had been a suitable place, the fear of infection for my cousins made it not to be thought of.

"Where would *you* like to go, Nurse?" I inquired one evening, as we all sat in the boudoir discussing the topic of the day.

"I should like to go wherever it's best for your good health, Master Reginald," was Nurse Bundle's answer, which, though admirable in its spirit, did not further the settlement of the matter we found it so difficult to decide.

"But where would you like to go for yourself?" I persisted. "Where would you go if it was you going away, and nobody else?"

"Well, my dear, if it was me just going away for myself, I think I should go to my sister's at Oakford."

This reply drew from me a catechism of questions about Oakford, and Nurse Bundle's sister, and Nurse Bundle's sister's husband, and their children; and when my father came to sit with me I had a long history of Oakford and Nurse Bundle's relatives at my fingers' ends, and was full of a new fancy, which was strong upon me, to go and stay for awhile at Oakford with Mr. and Mrs. Benjamin Buckle.

"Nurse says they sometimes let lodgings," I said; "and I should like Nurse to see her sister; and," I candidly added, "I should like to see her myself."

My father's uppermost wish was to please me; and as Oakford was known to be healthy, and the doctor favoured the proposition, it was decided according to my wishes. If we stayed long, my father was to go backwards and forwards, and he was to fetch us when we went away. His anxiety was still so great, and led him to watch me in a manner which fidgeted me so much, that I think the doctor was only too glad that the place should be sufficiently near to induce him to leave me to the care of Nurse Bundle.

We went by coach to Oakford. I was not allowed to sit outside on this journey. It was only a short one, however; and, truth to say, I did not feel strong enough for any feats of energy, and went meekly enough into that stuffy hole, the inside! Before following me, Nurse Bundle gave some directions to the driver, of a kind that could only be effectual in reference to a small place where everybody was known.

"Coachman! Oakford! And drop us at Mr. Buckle's, please, the saddler."

"High Street, isn't it?" said the fat coachman, looking down on Mrs. Bundle exactly as a parrot looks down from his perch.

"To be sure; only three doors below the 'Crown.'"

With which Mrs. Bundle gathered up her skirts, and her worsted workbag, and clambered into the coach.

There were two other "insides." One of these never spoke at all during the journey. The other only spoke once, and he seems to have been impelled thereto by a three hours' contemplation of the contrast between my slim, wasted little figure, and Nurse Bundle's portly person, as we sat opposite to him. He was a Scotchman, and I fancy "in business."

"You're weel matched to sit on the one side," was his remark.

Once, when I was feeling faint, he opened the window without my having spoken, and only acknowledged my thanks by a silent nod. When the coach stopped in the High Street of Oakford, and Nurse Bundle had descended, he so far relaxed, as he handed out me and the worsted workbag, as to indulge his national thirst for general information by the inquiring remark:

"You'll be staying at the 'Crown' the night, mem?"

"No, sir. We stop here," said Nurse Bundle.

I caught his keen blue eye at the window whilst the coach was delayed by the getting out of our luggage. I do not think he missed one feature of our welcome on the threshold of the saddler's shop.

I feel sure that Scotchmen do greatly profit by the habit they have of "absorbing into their constitutions," so to speak, all the facts of every kind that come within their ken. They "go in for general information," like the Tom Toddy in Mr. Kingsley's 'Water Babies;' but their hard heads have, fortunately, no likeness to turnips.

This, however, is a digression.

Mr. Benjamin Buckle, Mrs. Benjamin Buckle, Jemima Buckle, their daughter, Mr. Buckle's apprentice, and the "general girl," or maid-of-all-work, were all in the shop to receive us. I believe the cat was the only living creature in the house who was not there. But cats seldom exert themselves unnecessarily on behalf of other people, and she awaited our arrival upstairs. I had a severe if not undignified struggle with the string before I could get my hat off. Then I advanced, and, holding out my hand to Mr. Buckle, said,

"Mr. Buckle, I believe?"

"The same to you, sir, and a many of them," said Mr. Buckle, hastily; being, I fancy, rather put out by the touch of my frail hand, which was certainly very unlike the leather he handled daily. He saw his mistake, and added quickly,

"Your servant, sir. I hope your health's better, sir?"

"Very well, thank you," said I (all children make that answer, I think).

"What a little gentleman!" said Mrs. Buckle, in an audible "aside" to my nurse. She was as good-natured a woman as Mrs. Bundle herself, but with less brains. She lived in a chronic state of surprises and superlatives.

"You are Nurse's sister, aren't you, please?" I asked, going up to her, and once more tendering my hand. "I wanted to see you very much."

"Now just to think of that, Jemima! did you ever?" cried Mrs. Buckle.

"La!" said Jemima; in acknowledgment of which striking remark, I bent my head, and said,

"How do you do, Jemima?" adding, almost without an instant's pause, "Please take me away, Nurse! I am so very tired."

By one immediate and unbroken action, Mrs. Bundle cut her way through our hospitable friends and the scattered rolls of leather and other trade accessories in the shop, and conveyed me into an arm-chair in the sitting-room upstairs, where I sat, the tears running down my face for very weakness.

I had longed for the novelty of a residence above a saddler's shop; but now, too weary for new experiences, I was only conscious that the stairs were narrow, the room dingy and vulgar after the rooms at home, and as I wept I wished I had never come.

At this day, I am glad that I had the courtesy to restrain my feelings, and not to damp the delighted welcome of Nurse and her friends by an insulting avowal of my disappointment. I really was not a spoilt child; and indeed, the insolent and undisciplined egotism of many children "now-a-days," was not often tolerated by the past generation. As I sat silent and sad, Nurse Bundle ransacked her bag, muttering, "What a fool I be, to be sure!" and anon produced a flask of wine, from which she filled a wine-glass with a very big leg, which was one of the chimney ornaments. I emptied it in obedience to her orders, and in a few minutes my tears ceased, and I began to take a more cheerful view of the wallpaper and the antimacassars.

"What a pretty cat!" I said, at last. The said cat, a beauty, was lying on the hearthrug.

"Isn't it a beauty, love?" said Nurse Bundle; "and look, my dear, at your own little dog lying as good as gold in the rocking-chair, and not so much as looking at puss."

Rubens did not *quite* deserve this panegyric. He lay in his chair without touching puss, it is true; but he kept his eye firmly and constantly fixed upon her, only restrained from an attack by my known objection to such proceedings, and by the immovable composure of the good lady herself. Half a movement of encouragement on my part, half a movement of flight on the cat's, and Rubens would have been after her. All this was so plainly expressed in his attitude, that I burst out laughing. Rubens chose to take this as a sound to the chase, and only by the most peremptory orders could I induce him to keep quiet. As to the cat, I saw one convulsive twitch of the very tip of her tail, eloquent of wrath; otherwise she never moved.

"Now, my dear," said Mrs. Bundle, "suppose you come upstairs to bed, and get a good night's rest. I can hear Jemima a-shaking of the coals in the warming-pan now, on the stairs."

Warming-pans were not much used at home, and I was greatly interested in the brazen implement which Jemima wielded so dexterously.

"It's like an ironing cloth," was my comment when I got between the sheets. I had often warmed my hands on the table where Nurse ironed my collars at home.

Rubens duly came to bed; and I fell asleep, well satisfied on the whole with Oakford and the saddler's household.

# CHAPTER XI

## THE TINSMITH'S—THE BEAVER BONNETS—A FLAT IRON FOR A FARTHING—I FAIL TO SECURE A SISTER—RUBENS AND THE DOLL

Oakford was not a large town. It only boasted of one street, "to be called a street," as Mr. Buckle phrased it, though two or three lanes, with more or less pretentious rows of houses, and so forth, ran at right angles to the High Street. The High Street was a steep hill. It was tolerably broad, very clean, pebbled and picturesque. The "Crown Inn" was an old house with an historical legend attached to it. Several of the shops were also in very old houses, with overhanging upper stories and most comfortable window seats. Mr. Buckle's was one of these.

The air of the place was keen, but very healthy, and I seemed to gain strength with every hour of my stay. With strength, all my interest in the novelty of the situation woke afresh, and I was delighted with everything, but especially with the shop.

On the subject of the saddlery business, I must confess that a difference of opinion existed between myself and my excellent nurse. She jealously maintained my position as a "young gentleman" and lodger, against the familiarity into

Juliana Horatia Ewing

which the Buckles and I fell by common consent. She served my meals in separate state, and kept Jemima as well as herself in attendance on my wants. She made my sitting-room as comfortable as she could, and here it was her wish that I should sit, when in the house, "like a young gentleman." My wish, on the contrary, was to be in the shop, and as much as possible like a grown-up saddler. It did seem so delightful to be always working at that nice-smelling leather, and to be able to make for oneself unlimited straps, whips, and other masculine appendages. I was perfectly happy with spare fragments, cutting out miniature saddles and straps, stamping lines, punching holes, and mislaying the good saddler's tools in these efforts; whilst my thoughts were occupied with many a childish plan for inducing my father to apprentice me to the worthy Mr. Buckle.

I was a good deal taken with Mr. Buckle's apprentice, a rosy-cheeked young man, whose dress and manners I endeavoured as much as possible to imitate. I strutted in imitation of his style of walking down the High Street, and about this time Nurse Bundle was wont to say she "couldn't think what had come to" my hat, that it was "always stuck on one side." Pondering the history of Dick Whittington and the fair Alice, I said one day to Jemima Buckle,

"I suppose you and Andrew will marry, and when Mr. Buckle dies you will have the shop?"

"Me marry the 'prentice!" said Miss Jemima. And I discovered how little I knew of the shades of "caste" in Oakford.

Jemima used often to take me out when Nurse Bundle was otherwise engaged, and we were always very good friends. One day, I remember, she was going to a shop about half way up the High Street, and I obtained leave to go with her. Mrs. Bundle was busy superintending the cooking of some special delicacy for her "young gentleman's" dinner, and Jemima and I set forth on our errand. It was to a tinsmith's shop, where a bath had been ordered for my accommodation.

Ah! through how many years that steep street, with its clean, sunny stones, its irregular line of quaint old buildings, and the distant glimpse of big trees within palings into which it passed at the top, where the town touched the outskirts of some gentleman's place, has remained on my mind like a picture! Getting a little vague after a few years, and then perhaps a little altered, as fancy almost involuntarily supplied the defects of memory; but still that steep street, that tinsmith's shop—*the* features of Oakford!

I have since thought that Jemima must have had some special attraction to the tinsmith's, her errands there were so many, and took so much time. This occasion may be divided into three distinct periods. During the first, I waited in that state of vacant patience whereby one endures other people's shopping. During the second, I walked round all the cans, pans, colanders, and graters, and took a fancy to a tin mug. It was neither so valuable nor so handsome as the silver mug with dragon handles given me by my Indian godfather, but it was a novelty. When I looked closer, however, I found that it was marked, in plain figures, fourpence, which at that time was beyond my means; so I walked to the door, that I might solace the third period by looking out into the street. As I looked, there came down the hill a fine, large, sleek donkey, led by an old man-servant, and having on its back what is called a Spanish saddle, in which two little girls sat side by side, the whole party jogging quietly along at a foot's pace in the sunshine. I may say here that my experience of little girls had been almost entirely confined to my cousins, and that I was so overwhelmed and impressed by the loveliness of these two children, and by their quaint, queenly little ways, that time has not dimmed one line in the picture that they then made upon my mind. I can see them now as clearly as I saw them then, as I stood at the tinsmith's door in the High Street of Oakford—let me see, how many years ago? ("Never mind," says my wife; "go on with the story, my dear," and I go on.)

The child who looked the older, but was, as I afterwards discovered, the younger of the two, was also the less pretty. And yet she had a sweet little face, hair like spun gold, and blue-grey eyes with dark lashes. She wore a grey frock of some warm material, below which peeped her indoors dress of blue. The outer coat had a quaint cape like a coachman's, which was relieved by a broad white crimped frill round her throat. Her legs were cased in knitted gaiters of white wool, and her hands in the most comical miniatures of gloves. On her fairy head she wore a large bonnet of grey beaver, with a frill inside. (My wife explains that it was a "cap-front," adorned with little bunches of ribbon, and having a cap attached to it, the whole being put on separately before the bonnet. Details which seem to amuse my little daughters, and to have less interest for my sons.) But it was her sister who shone on my young eyes like a fairy vision. She looked too delicate, too brilliant, too utterly lovely, for anywhere but fairy-land. She ought to have been kept in tissue-paper, like the loveliest of wax dolls. Her hair was the true flaxen, the very fairest of the fair. The purity and vividness of the tints of red and white in her face I have never seen equalled. Her eyes were of speedwell blue, and looked as if they were meant to be always more or less brimming with tears. To say the truth, her face had not half the character which gave force to that of the other little damsel, but a certain helplessness about it gave it a peculiar charm. She was dressed exactly like the other, with one exception; her bonnet was of white beaver, and she became it like a queen.

At the tinsmith's door they stopped, and the old man-servant, after unbuckling a strap which seemed to support them in their saddle, lifted each little miss in turn to the ground. Once on the pavement, the little lady of the grey beaver shook herself out, and proceeded to straighten the disarranged overcoat of her companion, and then, taking her by the hand, the two clambered up the step into the shop. The tinsmith's shop boasted of two seats, and on to one of these she of the grey beaver with some difficulty climbed. The eyes of the other were fast filling with tears, when from her lofty perch the sister caught sight of the man-servant, who stood in the doorway, and she beckoned him with a wave of her tiny finger.

"Lift her up, if you please," she said, on his approach. And the other child was placed on the other chair.

The shopman appeared to know them, and though he smiled, he said very respectfully,

"What article can I show you this morning, ladies?"

The fairy-like creature in the white beaver, who had been fumbling in her miniature glove, now timidly laid a farthing on the counter, and then turning her back for very shyness on the shopman, raised one small shoulder, and inclining her head towards it, gave an appealing glance at her sister out of the pale-blue eyes. That little lady, thus appealed to, firmly placed another farthing on the board, and said in the tiniest but most decided of voices,

"TWO FLAT IRONS, IF YOU PLEASE."

Hereupon the shopman produced a drawer from below the counter, and set it before them. What it contained I was not tall enough to see, but out of it he took several tiny flat irons of triangular shape, and apparently made of pewter, or some alloy of tin. These the grey beaver examined and tried upon a corner of her cape with inimitable gravity and importance. At last she selected two, and keeping one for herself, gave the other to her sister.

"Is it a nice one?" the little white-beavered lady inquired.

"Very nice."

"*Kite* as nice as yours?" she persisted.

"Just the same," said the other, firmly. And having glanced at the corner to see that the farthings were both duly deposited, she rolled abruptly over on her seat, and scrambled off backwards, a manoeuvre which the other child accomplished with more difficulty. The coats and capes were then put tidy as before, and the two went out of the shop together hand in hand.

Then the old man-servant lifted them into the Spanish saddle, and buckled the strap, and away they went up the steep street, and over the brow of the hill, where trees and palings began to show, the beaver bonnets nodding together in consultation over the flat irons.

# CHAPTER XII

## THE LITTLE LADIES AGAIN—THE MEADS—THE DROWNED DOLL

"Mr. Buckle, sir, can you oblige me with eight farthings for twopence?"

I had closely copied this form of speech from the apprentice, whose ways, as I have said, I endeavoured in every way to imitate. Thus, twopence being at that time the extent of my resources, I went about for some days after my adventure at the tinsmith's with all my worldly wealth in my pocket in farthings, pondering many matters.

I began to have my doubts about saddlery as a profession. Truth to say, a want beyond the cutting and punching of leather had begun to stir within me. I wished for a sister. Somehow I had never desired to adopt one of my cousins in this relation, not even my dear friend Polly; but since I had seen the little lady in the white beaver, I felt how nice it would be to have such a sister to play with, as I had heard of other sisters and brothers playing together. Then I fancied myself showing her all my possessions at home, and begging the like for her from my indulgent father. I pictured the new interest which my old toys would derive from being exhibited to her. I thought I would beg for an exhibition of the magic lantern, for a garden for her like my own, and for several half-holidays. It delighted me to imagine myself presenting her with whatever she most admired, like some Eastern potentate or fairy godmother. But I could not connect her in my mind with the saddlery business. I felt that to possess so dainty and elegant a little lady as a sister was incompatible with an apprenticeship to Mr. Buckle.

Meanwhile I kept watch on the High Street from Mr. Buckle's door. One morning I saw the donkey, the man, the Spanish saddle, and the beaver bonnets come over the brow of the hill, and I forthwith ran to Nurse Bundle, and begged leave to go alone to the tinsmith's, and invest one of my eight farthings in a flat iron. It was only a few yards off, and she consented; but, as I had to submit to be dressed, by the time I got there the little ladies were already in the shop, and seated on the two chairs. My fairy beauty looked round as I came in, and recognizing me, gave a little low laugh, and put her head on her own shoulder, and then peeped again, smiling so sweetly that I fairly loved her. The other was too deeply engaged in poking and fumbling for farthings in her glove to permit herself to be distracted by anything or anybody. This process was so slow that the shopman came up to me and asked what I wanted. I took a well-warmed farthing from the handful I carried, and laid it on the counter, saying—

"A flat iron, if you please."

He put several before me, and after making a show of testing them on the end of my comforter, I selected one at random. I know that I did not do it with half the air which the little grey-beavered lady had thrown over the proceeding, but I hardly deserved the scornful tone in which she addressed no one in particular with the remark, "He has no business with flat irons. He's only a boy."

She evidently expected no reply, for without a pause she proceeded to count out five farthings on to the counter, saying as she did so, "A frying-pan, a gridiron, a dish, and two plates, if you please." On which, to my astonishment, miniature specimens of these articles, made of the same material as the flat irons, were produced from the box whence those had come. I was so bewildered by the severity of the little lady's remarks, and the wonderful things which she obtained for her farthings, that I dropped my remaining seven on to the shop floor, and was still grubbing for them in the dust, when the children having finished their shopping, came backwards off the seats as usual. They passed me in the doorway, hand in hand. The little lady with the white beaver was next to me, and as she passed she gave a shy glance, and her face dimpled all over into smiles. Unspeakably pleased by her recognition, I abandoned my farthings to their fate, and jumping up, I held out my dusty hand to the little damsel, saying hastily but as civilly as I could, "How do you do? I hope you're pretty well. And oh, please, *will* you be my sister?"

Having once begun, I felt quite equal to a full explanation of my position and the prospect of toys and treats before us both. I was even prepared, in the generous excitement of the moment to endow my new sister with a joint partnership in the possession of Rubens, and was about to explain all the advantages the little lady would derive from having me for a brother, when I was stopped by the changed expression on her pretty face.

I suppose my sudden movement had startled her, for her smiles vanished in a look of terror, as she clung to her companion, who opened wide her eyes, and shaking her grey beaver vehemently, said, "We don't know you, Boy!"

Then they fled to the side of the old man-servant as fast as

　Juliana Horatia Ewing

their white-gaitered legs would carry them.

I watered the dusty floor of the shop with tears of vexation as I resumed my search for the farthings, and having found them I went back to the saddler's, pounding them in my hot hand, and bitterly disappointed.

I don't suppose that Rubens understood the feelings which gave an extra warmth to my caresses, as I hugged him in my arms, exclaiming,

"*You* aren't afraid of me, you dear thing!"

But he responded sympathetically, both with tongue and tail.

I had not frightened the little ladies away from the High Street, it seemed. I saw them again two days later. They had been out as usual, and some trifling mischance having happened to the Spanish saddle, they called at Mr. Buckle's door for repairs. I was in the shop, and could see the two little maidens as they sat hanging over their strap, with a doll dressed very much like themselves between them. I crept nearer to the door, where the quick grey eyes of the younger one caught sight of me, and I heard her say in her peculiarly trenchant tones—

"Why, there's that Boy again!"

I slipped a little to one side, and took up a tool and a bit of leather with a pretence of working, hoping to be out of sight, and yet to be able to look at the little white-beavered fairy, for whom my fancy was in no way abated. But her keen-eyed sister saw me still, and her next remark rang out with uncompromising distinctness—

"He's in the shop still. He's working. He must be a shop-boy!"

I dropped the tools, and rushed away to my sitting-room. My mortification was complete, and it was of a kind that Rubens could not understand. Fortunately for me, he simply went with my humour, without being particular as to the reason of it, like the tenderest of women.

A day or two afterwards I went out with Rubens and Jemima Buckle for a walk. Our way home lay through some flat green meads, crossed by a stream, which, in its turn, was crossed by a little rustic bridge. As we came into these fields we met a man whose face seemed familiar, though I could not at first recall where I had seen him. Afterwards I remembered that he was the tinsmith, and Jemima stayed to chat with him for a few minutes, but Rubens and I strolled on.

It seemed an odd coincidence that, a few seconds after meeting the tinsmith, I should meet the little white-beavered lady. She was crossing the bridge. Her sister was not with her, nor the donkey, nor the man-servant. She was walking with a nurse, and she carried a big doll in her arms. The doll, as I have said before, was "got up" wonderfully like its mistress. It had a miniature coat and cape and frills, it had leggings, it had a white plush bonnet (so my wife enables me to affirm), it had hair just the colour of the little lady's locks.

As she crossed the bridge, she seemed much pleased by the running of the water beneath her feet, and saying, "Please let Dolly 'ook," in her pretty broken tones, she pushed her doll through the rustic work, holding it by its sash. But, alas! the doll was heavy, and the sash insecurely fastened. It gave way, and the doll plunged into the stream.

Once more the sweet little face was convulsed by a look of terror and distress. As the doll floated out on the other side of the bridge, she shrieked and wrung her hands. As for me, I ran down to the edge of the stream, calling Rubens after me, and pointing to the doll. Only too glad of an excuse for a plunge, in he dashed, and soon brought the unfortunate miss to shore by one of her gaitered legs. It was with some triumph that I carried the dripping doll to its little mistress, and heard the nurse admonish her to—

"Thank the young gentleman, my dear."

I have often since heard of faces "like an April sky," but I never saw one which did so resemble it in being by turns bright and overcast, with tears and smiles struggling together, and fear and pleased recognition, as the face of the little blonde in the white beaver bonnet. It was she who held out her hand this time, and as I took it she said, "'ank you 'erry much."

"It was Rubens' doing, not mine," said I. "Rubens! shake hands, sir!"

But the little lady was frightened. She shrank away from the warm greeting of Rubens, and I was obliged to shake hands with him myself to satisfy his feelings.

The nursemaid had been wringing out the doll's clothes for the little lady, but now they moved on together.

"Dood-bye!" said the little lady, smiling and waving her hand. I waved mine, and then Jemima, having parted with the tinsmith, came up, and we went home.

I never saw the beaver bonnets again.

# CHAPTER XIII

## POLLY—THE PEW AND THE PULPIT—THE FATE OF THE FLAT IRON

By the time that my father came to fetch us away, I was wonderfully improved in health and strength. I even wanted to go back outside the coach; but this was not allowed.

I did not forget the little lady in the white beaver, even after my return to Dacrefield. I was fond of drawing, and I made what seemed to me a rather striking portrait of her (at least as to colouring), and wore it tied by a bit of string round my neck. It is unromantic to have to confess that it fell at last into the washhand basin, and was reduced to pulp.

I brought my farthing flat-iron home with me, and it was for long a favourite plaything. I used to sprinkle corners of my pocket-handkerchief with water, as I had seen Nurse Bundle "damp fine things" before ironing them. But after all, "play" of this kind is dull work played alone. I was very glad when Polly came.

It was a few weeks after our return that my father proposed to ask Cousin Polly to pay us a visit. I think my aunt had said something in a letter about her not being well, and the visit was supposed to be for the benefit of her health.

She was not ill for long at Dacrefield. My "lessons" were of a very slight description as yet, and we spent most of our time out of doors. The fun of showing Polly about the farm and grounds was quite as satisfactory as any that my dream of the flaxen-haired sister had promised. I was quite prepared to yield to Cousin Polly in all things as before; but she, no doubt in deference to my position as host, met me halfway with unusual affability and graciousness. Country life exactly suited her. I think she was profoundly happy exploring the garden, making friends with the cows and horses, feeding the rabbits and chickens, and "playing at haunted castles" in the barn.

Her vigour and daring when we climbed trees together were the objects of my constant admiration. Tree-climbing was Polly's favourite amusement, and the various fancies she "pretended" in connection with it, did credit to her imaginative powers. Sometimes she "pretended" to be Jack in the Beanstalk; sometimes she pretended to be at the mast-head of a ship at sea; sometimes to be in an upper story of a fairy-house; sometimes to be escaping from a bear; sometimes (with recollections of London) to be the bear himself on a pole, or a monkey in the Zoological Gardens; or to be on the top of the Monument or of St. Paul's. Our most common game, however, was the time-honoured drama of "houses." Each branch constituted a story, and we used to emulate each other in our exploits of high climbing, with a formula that ran thus:—

"Now I'm in the area" (the lowest branch). "Now I'm on the dining-room floor" (the next), and so on, ending with, "And now I'm the very poor person in the garret."

There were two trees which stood near each other, of about equal difficulty.

We used each to climb one, and as we started together, the one who first became the "very poor person in the garret" was held to be the winner of the game.

We were not allowed to climb trees on Sunday, which was a severe exercise of Polly's principles. One Sunday afternoon, however, much to my amazement, she led me away down the shrubbery, saying,

"My dear Regie! I've found two trees which I'm sure we may climb on Sundays." Much puzzled, I nevertheless yielded to her, being quite accustomed to trust all her proceedings.

I was not enlightened by the appearance of the trees, which were very much like others as to their ladder-like peculiarities. They were old Portugal laurels which had been cut in a good deal at various times. They looked very easy to climb, and did not seem to boast many "stories." I did not see anything about them adapted for Sunday amusement in particular.

But Polly soon explained herself.

"Look here, Regie," said she; "this tree has got three beautiful branches, one for the clerk, one for the reading-desk, and one for the pulpit. I'm going to get into the top one and preach you a sermon; and you're to sit in that other tree—it makes a capital pew. I'm sure it's quite a Sunday game," added Polly, mounting to the pulpit with her accustomed energy.

I seated myself in the other tree; and Polly, after consuming some time in "settling herself," appeared to be ready; but she still hesitated, and finally burst out laughing.

"I beg your pardon," she added, rubbing her hands over her

Juliana Horatia Ewing

laughing mouth, and composing herself. "Now I'm going to begin." But she still giggled, which led me to say—

"Never mind the text, as you're laughing. Begin at once without."

"Very well," said Polly.

There was another break down, and then she seemed fairly grave.

"My dear brethren," she began.

"There's only one of us," I ventured to observe.

"Now, Regie, you mustn't speak. The congregation never speaks to the clergyman when he's preaching."

"It's such a small congregation," I pleaded.

"Well, then, I won't preach at all, if you go on like that," said Polly.

But, as I saw that she was getting cross, and as I had no intention of offending her, I apologized, and begged her to proceed with her sermon. So she began again accordingly—

"My dear brethren."

But here she paused; and after a few moments of expectation on my part, and silence on Polly's, she said—

"Is your pew comfortable, Regie dear?"

"Very," said I. "How do you like the pulpit?"

"Very much indeed," said Polly; "but I don't think I can preach without a cushion. Suppose we talk."

Thus the sermon was abandoned; and as Polly refused to let me try my luck in the pulpit, she remained at a considerably higher level than I was. At last I became impatient of this fact, and began to climb higher.

"Stop!" cried Polly; "you mustn't leave your pew."

"I'm going into the gallery," a happy thought enabled me to say.

Polly made no answer. She seemed to be meditating some step; and presently I saw her scramble down to the ground in her own rapid fashion.

"Regie dear, will you promise not to get into my pulpit till I come back?" she begged.

I gave the promise; and, without answering my questions as to what she was going to do, she sped off towards the house. In about five minutes she returned with something held in the skirt of her frock, which seemed greatly to incommode her in climbing. At last she reached the pulpit, but she did not stay there. Up and on she went, much hindered by her burden.

"Polly! Polly!" I cried. "You mustn't go higher than the pulpit. You know it isn't fair. The pulpit is the top one, and you must stay there. The clergyman never goes into the gallery."

"I'm not going into the gallery," she gasped; and on she went to the topmost of the large branches. There she paused, and from her lap she drew forth the dinner-bell.

"I'm in the belfry," she shouted in tones of triumph, "and I'm going to ring the bell for service."

Which she accordingly did, with such a hearty goodwill that Nurse Bundle and several others of the household came out to see what was the matter. My father laughed loudly, but Mrs. Bundle was seriously displeased.

"Master Reginald would never have thought of no such thing on a Sunday afternoon but for you, Miss Polly," she said, with a partiality for her "own boy" which offended my sense of justice.

"I climbed a tree too, Nurse," I said, emphatically.

"And it was only a Sunday kind of climbing," Polly pleaded. But Nurse Bundle refused to see the force of Polly's idea; we were ignominiously dismissed to the nursery, and thenceforward were obliged, as before, to confine our tree-climbing exploits to the six working days of the week.

And these Portugal laurels bore the names of the Pulpit and the Pew ever afterwards.

\* \* \* \* \*

I showed my flat iron to Polly, and she was so much pleased with it that I greatly regretted that I had only brought away this one from Oakford. I should have given it to her, but for its connection with the little white-beavered lady.

We both played with it; and at a suggestion of Polly's, we gave quite a new character to our "wash" (or rather "ironing," for we omitted the earlier processes of the laundry). We used to cut small models of clothes out of white paper, and then iron them with the farthing iron. How nobly that domestic implement did its duty till the luckless day when Polly became uneasy because we did not "put it down to the fire to get hot!"

"Nurse doesn't like us to play with fire," I conscientiously reminded her.

"It's not playing with fire; it's only putting the iron on the hob," said Polly.

And to this unworthy evasion I yielded, and—my arm being longer than Polly's—put the flat iron on the top bar of the nursery grate with my own hand. Whilst the iron was heating we went back to our scissors and paper.

"You cut out a few more white petticoats, Regie dear," said Polly, "and I will make an iron-holder;" with which she calmly cut several inches off the end of her sash, and began to fold it for the purpose.

Aunt Maria's nursery discipline was firm, but her own nature was independent, almost to aggressiveness; and Polly inherited enough of the latter to more than counteract the repression of the former. Thus all Cousin Polly's proceedings were very direct, and, if necessary, daring. When she cut her sash, I exclaimed—"My dear Polly!" just as Uncle Ascott was wont at times to cry—"My dear Maria!"

"I'd nothing else to make it of," said Polly, calmly. "It's better than cutting up my pocket-handkerchief, for it only shortens it a little, and Mamma often cuts the ends a little when our sashes ravel. How many petticoats have you done, dear?"

"Four," said I.

"Well, we've three skirts. Those long strips will do for Uncle

Reginald's neckties. You can cut that last sheet into two pieces, and we'll pretend they're tablecloths. And then I think you'd better fetch the iron. Here's the holder."

"Oh! Polly dear! It is such fun!" I cried; but as I drew near to the fireplace the words died away on my lips. My flat iron was gone.

At first I thought it had fallen on to the hearth; but looking nearer I saw a blob or button of lead upon the bar of the grate. There was no resisting the conviction which forced itself upon me: my flat iron was melted.

Polly was much distressed. Doubly so because she had been the cause of the misfortune. As we were examining the shapeless lump of metal, she said, "It's like a little lump of silver that Miss Blomfield has hanging to her watch chain;" which determined me to have a hole made through the remains of my flat iron, and do the same.

"Papa has promised me a watch next birthday," I added.

Polly and I were very happy and merry together; but her visit came to an end at last. Aunt Maria came to fetch her. She had brought her down when she came, but had only stayed one night. On this occasion she stayed from Saturday to Monday. Aunt Maria never allowed any of the girls to travel alone, and they were never allowed to visit without her at any but relations' houses. One consequence of which was, that when they grew up, and were large young women with large noses, they were the most helpless creatures at a railway-station that I ever beheld.

Whilst Aunt Maria was with us, she "spoke seriously," as it is called, to my father about my education. I think she was shocked to discover how thoroughly Polly and I had been "running wild" during Polly's visit. Whether my father had given any rash assent to proposals for our studying together, which Aunt Maria may have made at her last visit, or not, I do not know. Anyway, my aunt seemed to be shocked, and enlarged to my father on the waste of time involved in allowing me to run wild so long. My father was apt to "take things easy," and I fancy he made some vague promises as to my education, which satisfied my aunt for the time. Polly and I parted with much grief on both sides. Aunt Maria took her back to her lessons, and I was left to my loneliness.

I felt Polly's loss very much, especially as my father happened to be a good deal engaged just then, and Nurse Bundle busy superintending some new arrangements in our nursery premises. I think she missed Polly herself; we had not been so quiet for some weeks. We almost felt it dull.

"Of course a country place *is* very quiet," Mrs. Bundle said one evening to the housekeeper, with whom we were having tea for a change. "Anybody feels it that has ever lived in a town, where people is always dropping in."

"What's 'dropping in,' Nurse?" I asked.

"Well, my dear, just calling in at anybody's house, and sitting down in a friendly way, to exchange the weather and pass time like."

"That must be very nice," I said.

"Like as if we was in Oakford," Mrs. Bundle continued, "and I could drop in, as it might be this afternoon, and take a seat in my sister's and ask after their good healths."

"I wish we could," said I.

The idea fermented in my brain, as ideas were wont to do, in the large share of solitary hours that fell to my lot. The result of it was the following adventure.

# CHAPTER XIV

## RUBENS AND I "DROP IN" AT THE RECTORY—GARDENS AND GARDENERS—MY FATHER COMES FOR ME

One fine morning, when my father was busy with the farm-bailiff, and Mrs. Bundle was "sorting" some clothes, I took my best hat from the wardrobe, deliberately, and with some difficulty put on a clean frill, fastened my boots, and calling Rubens after me, set forth from the hall unnoticed by any of the family.

Rubens jumped up at me in an inquiring fashion as we went along. He could not imagine where we were going. I knew quite well. I was making for the Rectory, the road to which I knew. I had often thought I should like to go and see Mr. Andrewes, and Mrs. Bundle's remarks to the housekeeper had suggested to me the idea of calling upon him. We were near neighbours, though we did not live in a town. I resolved to "drop in" at the Rectory.

It was a lovely morning, and Rubens and I quite enjoyed our walk. He became so much excited that it was with difficulty that I withheld him from chasing the ducks on the pond in Mr. Andrewes' farm-yard, as we went through it. (The parson had a little farm attached to his Rectory.) Then I with difficulty unlatched the heavy gate leading into the drive, and fastened it again with the scrupulous care of a country squire's son. The grounds were exquisitely kept. Mr. Andrewes was a first-rate gardener and a fair farmer. That neatness, without which the brightest flowers will not "show themselves" (as gardeners say), did full justice to every luxuriant shrub, and set off the pale, delicately-beautiful border of snowdrops and crocuses which edged the road, and the clumps of daffodil, polyanthus, and primrose flowers dotted hither and thither. I was not surprised to hear the chorus of birds above my head, for it was one of the parson's "oddities" that he would have no birds shot on his premises.

When I came into the flower-garden, there was more exquisite neatness, and more bright spring flowers, thinly scattered in comparison with summer blossoms, but shining brightly against the rich dark mould. And on the turf were lying gardening-tools, and busy among the tools and flower-beds were two men—the Rev. Reginald Andrewes and his gardener. It took me several seconds to distinguish master from man. They were both in straw hats and shirt sleeves, but I recognised the parson by his trousers. His hat was the older of the two, and not by any means "canonical." Having found him, I went up to the bed where he was busy, and sat down on the grass near him, without speaking. (I was accustomed to respect my father's "busy" moments, and yet to be with him.) Rubens followed my example, and sat down in silence also. He had smelt the parson before, and wagged his tail faintly as he saw him. But he reserved his opinion of the gardener, and seemed rather disposed to growl when he touched the wheelbarrow.

"Bless me!" said Mr. Andrewes, who was startled, as he well might be, by my appearance. "Why, my dear boy, how are you?"

"Very well, thank you," said I, getting up and offering my hand; "I've dropped in."

"Dear me!" said Mr. Andrewes; "I mean, I'm very glad to see you! Won't you come in? You mustn't sit on the grass."

"What a pretty garden you have!" I said, as we walked slowly towards the house. Mr. Andrewes turned round.

"Well, pretty well. It amuses me, you know," he said, with the mock humility of a real horticulturist. And he looked round his garden with an unmistakable glance of pride and affection. "Have you a garden, Reginald?" he inquired.

"Yes," I said. "At least, I've two beds and a border. The beds are shaped like an R and a D. But I haven't touched them since I was ill. The gardener tidied them up when I was at Oakford, and I think he has dug up all my plants. At least I couldn't find the Bachelor's Button, nor the London Pride, nor the Pansies, and I saw the Lavender-bush on the rubbish-heap."

"So they do—so they always do!" said the parson, excitedly. "The only way is to keep in the garden with them, and let nothing go into the wheelbarrow but what you see.—Jones! you may go to your dinner. I watch Jones like a dragon, but he sweeps up a tap-root now and then, all the same; and yet he's better than most of them. Some flowers are especially apt to take leave of one's beds and borders," Mr. Andrewes went on. He was talking to himself rather than to me by this time. "Fraxinellas, double-grey primroses, ay, and the pink and white ones too. And hepaticas, red, blue, and white."

"What are hepaticas like?" I asked.

"Let me show you," said Mr. Andrewes, crossing the garden.

Juliana Horatia Ewing

"Look here! there are the pretty little things. I have seen them growing wild in Canada—single ones, that is. The leaves are of a dull green, and when they fade, the whole plant is hardly to be distinguished from Mother Earth—at least, not by a gardener's eye. If you will promise me not to let the gardener meddle with them, unless you are there to look after him, I will give you plants for your beds and borders, my boy."

"Oh, thank you," I said; "I like gardening very much. I should like to garden like you. I've got a spade, and a hoe, and a fork, and I had a rake, but it's lost. But I know papa will give me another; and I can tidy my own beds, so the gardener need not touch them; and if there was a wheelbarrow small enough for me to wheel, I could take my weeds away myself, you know."

And I chattered on about my garden, for, like other children, I was apt to "take up" things very warmly, in imitation of other people; and Mr. Andrewes had already fired my imagination with dreams of a little garden in perfect order and beauty, and tended by my own hands alone; and as I talked of my garden, the parson talked of his, and so we wandered from border to border, finding each other very good company, Rubens walking demurely at our heels. A great many of Mr. Andrewes' remarks, though I am sure they were very instructive, were beyond my power of understanding; but as he closed each lecture on the various flowers by a promise of a root, a cutting, a sucker, a seedling, or a bulb, as the case might be, I was an attentive and well-satisfied listener. I much admired some daffodils, and Mr. Andrewes at once began to pick a bunch of them for me.

"Isn't it a pity to pick them?" I said, politely.

"My dear Regie," said Mr. Andrewes, "if ever you see

anybody with a good garden of flowers who grudges picking them for his friends, you may be quite sure he has not learnt half of what his flowers can teach him. Flowers are generous enough. The more you take from them the more they give. And yet I have seen people with beds glowing with geraniums, and trees laden with roses, who grudged to pluck them, not knowing that they would bloom all the better and more luxuriantly for being culled."

"Do daffodils flower better when the flowers are picked off?" I asked, having my full share of the childish propensity for asking awkward and candid questions. Mr. Andrewes laughed.

"Well, no. I must confess they are not quite like geraniums in this respect. And spring flowers are so few and so precious, one may be excused for not quite cutting them like summer flowers. But it wouldn't do only to be generous when it costs one nothing. Eh, Regie?"

I laughed and said "No," which was what I was expected to say, and thanked the parson for the daffodils. He pulled out his watch.

"My dear boy, it's luncheon time. Will you come in and have something to eat with me?"

I hesitated; Mrs. Bundle had not spoken of any meal in connection with the ceremony of "dropping in," but, on the other hand, I should certainly like to lunch at the Rectory, I thought. And, indeed, I was hungry.

"Oh, you must come," said Mr. Andrewes, leading me away without waiting for an answer. "I'm sure you must be hungry, and the dog too. What's his name, eh?"

"Rubens," said I.

"Does he paint?" Mr. Andrewes inquired. But as I knew nothing of Painter Peter Paul Rubens or his works, I was only puzzled, and said he knew a good many tricks which I had taught him.

"We'll see if he can beg for chicken-bones," said the parson, hospitably; and indoors we went. Mr. Andrewes said grace, though not in the words to which I was accustomed, and we sat down together, Rubens lying by my chair. I endeavoured to conduct myself with the strictest propriety, and I believe succeeded, except for the trifling mischance of spilling some bread-sauce on to my jacket. Mr. Andrewes saw this, however, and wanted to fasten a table-napkin round me, to which I objected.

"Too like a pinafore, eh?" said he, with a sly laugh.

"I don't think I ought to wear pinafores now," I said, in a grave and injured tone. "Leo Damer doesn't, and he's not much older than I am. But I think," I added, candidly, "he rather does as he likes, because he's got nobody to look after him."

The parson laughed, and then gave a heavy sigh.

"I wish my mother could come back, and tie a pinafore round my neck!" he exclaimed, abruptly. Then I believe he suddenly remembered that I had lost my mother and was vexed with himself for his hasty speech. I saw nothing inconsiderate in the remark, however, and only said,

"Is your mother dead?"

"Yes, my boy. Many years ago," said Mr. Andrewes.

"Did your father marry anybody else?" I inquired.

"My father died before my mother."

"Dear me," said I; "how very sad! Leo's father and mother died together. They were drowned in his father's yacht." I was in the middle of a history of my friend Leo, and of my visit to London, when a bell pealed loudly through the house.

"Somebody's in a hurry," said Mr. Andrewes; "that's the front-door bell."

In three minutes the dining-room door was opened, and the servant announced "Mr. Dacre." It would be untrue to say that I did not feel a little guilty when my father walked into the room. And yet I had not really thought there was "any harm" in my expedition. I think I was chiefly annoyed by the ignominious end of it. It was trying, after "dropping in" and "taking luncheon" like a grown-up gentleman, to be fetched home as a lost child.

"What could make you run away like this, Regie?" said my poor bewildered parent. "Mrs. Bundle is nearly mad with fright. It was very naughty of you. What were you thinking of?"

"I thought I would drop in," I explained. And in the pause resulting from my father's astonishment at my absurd and old-fashioned demeanour, I proceeded with Nurse Bundle's definition as well as I could recollect it in my confusion, and speak it for impending tears. "So I came, and Rubens came, and Mr. Andrewes was in the garden, and we sat down, to change the weather, and pass time like, and Mr. Andrewes was in the garden, and he gave me some flowers, and Mr. Andrewes asked me in, and I came in, and he gave me some luncheon and he asked Rubens to have some bones, and—"

"'Change the weather and pass time like,'" muttered my father. "Servants' language! oh, dear!"

In my vexation with things in general, and with the strong feeling within me that I was in the wrong, I seized upon the first grievance that occurred to me as an excuse for fretfulness, and once more quoted Nurse Bundle.

"It's so very quiet at home," I whimpered, with tears in my eyes, which had really no sort of connection with the dulness of the Hall, or with anything whatever but offended pride and vexation on my part.

Ah! How many a stab one gives in childhood to one's parents' tenderest feelings! I did not mean to be ungrateful, and I had no measure of the pain my father felt at this hint of the insufficiency of all he did for my comfort and pleasure at home. Mr. Andrewes knew better, and said, hastily,

"Just the love of novelty, Mr. Dacre. We have been children ourselves."

My father sighed, and sitting down, drew me towards him with one hand, stroking Rubens with the other, in acknowledgment of his greeting and wagging tail. Then I saw that he was hurt. Indeed, I fancied tears were in his eyes as he said,

"So poor Papa and home are too dull—too quiet, eh, Regie? And yet Papa does all he can for his boy."

My fit of ill-temper was gone in a moment, and I flung my arms round my father's neck—Rubens taking flying leaps to join in the embrace, after a fashion common with dogs, and decidedly dangerous to eyes, nose, and ears. And as I kissed my father, and was kissed by Rubens, I gave a candid account of my expedition. "No, dear papa. It wasn't that. Only Nurse said country places were quiet, and in towns people dropped in, and passed time, and changed the weather, and if she was in Oakford she would drop in and see her sister. And so I said it would be very nice. And so I thought this morning that Rubens and I would drop in and see Mr. Andrewes. And so we did; and we didn't tell because we wanted to come alone, for fun."

With this explanation the fullest harmony was restored; and my father sat down whilst Mr. Andrewes and I finished our luncheon and Rubens had his. I gave an account of the garden in terms glowing enough to satisfy the pride of the warmest horticulturist, and my father promised a new rake, and drank a glass of sherry to the success of my "gardening without a gardener."

But as we were going away I overheard him saying to Mr. Andrewes,

"All the same, a boy can't be with a nurse for ever. She has every good quality, except good English. And he is not a baby now. One forgets how time passes. I must see about a tutor."

## CHAPTER XV

## NURSE BUNDLE IS MAGNANIMOUS—MR. GRAY— AN EXPLANATION WITH MY FATHER

Naturally enough, I did my best to give Nurse Bundle a faithful account of my attempt to realize her idea of "dropping in," with all that came of it. My garden projects, the arrival of my father, and all that he said and did on the occasion. From my childish and confused account, I fancy that Nurse Bundle made out pretty correctly the state of the case. Being a "grown-up person," she probably guessed, without difficulty, the meaning of my father's concluding remarks. I think a good, faithful, tender-hearted nurse, such as she was, must suffer with some of a mother's feelings, when it is first decided that "her boy" is beyond petticoat government. Nurse Bundle cried so bitterly over this matter, that my most chivalrous feelings were roused, and I vowed that "Papa shouldn't say things to vex my dear Nursey." But Mrs. Bundle was very loyal.

"My dear," said she, wiping her eyes with her apron, "depend upon it, whatever your papa settles on is right. He knows what's suitable for a young gentleman; and it's only likely as a young gentleman born and bred should outgrow to be beyond what an old woman like me can do for him. Though there's no tutors nor none of them will ever love you better than poor Nurse Bundle, my deary. And there's no one ever has loved you better, my dear, nor ever will—always excepting your dear mamma, dead and gone."

All this stirred my feelings to the uttermost, and I wept too, and vowed unconquerable fidelity to Nurse Bundle, and (despite her remonstrances) unconquerable aversion from the tutor that was to be. I furthermore renewed my proposals of marriage to Mrs. Bundle,—the wedding to take place "when I should be old enough."

This set her off into fits of laughing; and having regained her good spirits, she declared that "she wouldn't have, no, not a young squire himself, unless he were eddicated accordingly;" and this, it was evident could only be brought about through the good offices of a tutor. And to the prospective tutor (though he was to be her rival) she was magnanimously favourable, whilst I, for my part, warmly opposed the very thought of him. But neither her magnanimity nor my unreasonable objections were put to the test just then.

Several days had passed since I and Rubens "dropped in" at the Rectory, and I was one morning labouring diligently at my garden, when I saw Mr. Andrewes, in his canonical coat and shoes, coming along the drive, carrying something in his hand which puzzled me. As he came nearer, however, I perceived that it was a small wheelbarrow, gaily painted red within and green without. At a respectful distance behind him walked Jones, carrying a garden-basket full of plants on his head.

Both the wheelbarrow and the plants were for me—a present from the good-natured parson. He was helping me to plant the flower-roots, and giving me a lecture on the sparing use of the wheelbarrow, when my father joined us, and I heard him say to Mr. Andrewes, "I should like a word with you, when you are at liberty."

I do not know what made me think that they were talking about me. I did, however, and watched them anxiously, as they passed up and down the drive in close consultation. At last I heard Mr. Andrewes say—

"The afternoon would suit me best; say an hour after luncheon."

This remark closed the conversation, and they came back to me. But I had overheard another sentence from Mr. Andrewes' lips, which filled me with disquiet,

"I know of one that will just suit you; a capital little fellow."

So the tutor was actually decided upon. "'A capital little fellow.' That means a nasty fussy little man!" I cried to myself. "I hate him!"

For the rest of that day, and all the next, I worried myself with thoughts of the new tutor. On the following morning, I was standing near one of the lodges with my father, looking at some silver pheasants, when Mr. Andrewes rode by, and called to my father.

Now, living as I did, chiefly with servants, and spending much more of my leisure than was at all desirable between the stables and the housekeeper's room, my sense of honour on certain subjects was not quite so delicate as it ought to have been. With all their many merits, uneducated people and servants have not—as a class—strict ideas on absolute truthfulness and honourable trustworthiness in all matters. A large part of the plans, hopes, fears, and quarrels of uneducated people are founded on what has been overheard by folk who were not intended to hear it, and on what has been told again by those to whom a matter was told in confidence. Nothing is a surer mark of good breeding and careful "upbringing" (as the Scotch call it) than delicacy on those little points which are trusted to one's honour. But refinement in such matters is easily blunted if one lives much with people who think any little meanness fair that is not found out. I really saw no harm in trying to overhear all that I could of the conversation between my father and Mr. Andrewes, though I was aware, from their manner, that I was not meant to hear it. I lingered near my father, therefore, and pretended to be watching the pheasants, for a certain instinct made me feel that I should not like my father to see me listening. He was one of those highly, scrupulously honourable gentlemen, before whose face it was impossible to do or say anything unworthy or mean.

He spoke in low tones, so that I lost most of what he said; but the parson's voice was a peculiarly clear one, and though he lowered it, I heard a good deal.

"I saw him yesterday," was Mr. Andrewes' first remark.

("That's the tutor," thought I.)

My father's answer I lost; but I caught fragments of Mr. Andrewes' next remarks, which were full of information on this important matter.

"Quite young, good-tempered—little boy so fond of him, nothing would have induced them to part with him; but they were going abroad."

Which sounded well; but I suspected the parson of a good deal of officious advice in a long sentence, of which I only caught the words, "Can't begin too early."

I felt convinced, too, that I heard something about the "use of the whip," which put me into a fever of indignation. Just as Mr. Andrewes was riding off, my father asked some question, to which the reply was—"Gray."

My head was so full of the tutor that I could not enjoy the stroll with my father as usual, and was not sorry to get back to Nurse Bundle, to whom I confided all that I had heard about my future teacher.

"He's a nasty little man," said I, "not a nice tall gentleman like Papa or Mr. Andrewes. And Mr. Andrewes saw him yesterday. And Mr. Andrewes says he's young. And he says he's good-natured; but then what makes him use whips? And his name is Mr. Gray. And he says the other little boy was very fond of him, but I don't believe it," I continued, breaking down at this point into tears, "and they've gone abroad (sobs) and I wish—boohoo! boohoo—they'd taken *him*!"

With some trouble Nurse Bundle found out the meaning of my rather obscure speech. Her wrath at the thought of a whip in connection with her darling was quite as great as my own. But she persisted in taking a hopeful view of Mr. Gray, and trusting loyally to my father's judgment, and she succeeded in softening my grief for the time.

When I came down to dessert that evening I pretended to be quite happy and comfortable, and to have nothing on my mind. But happily few children are clever at pretending what is not true, and as I was constantly thinking about "that dreadful tutor," and puzzling over the scraps of conversation I had heard to see if anything more could be made out of them, my father soon found out that something was amiss.

"What is the matter, Regie?" he asked.

"Nothing, Father," I replied, with a very poor imitation of cheerfulness and no approach to truth.

"My dear boy," said my father, frowning slightly (a thing I always dreaded), "do not say what is untrue, for any reason. If you do not want to tell me what troubles you, say, 'I'd rather not tell you, please,' like a man, and I will not persecute you about it. But don't say there is nothing the matter when your little head is quite full of something that bothers you very much. As I said, I will not press you, but as I love you, and wish to help you in every way I can, I think you had better tell me."

Now, though I had really not thought I was doing wrong in listening to the conversation I was not meant to hear, a *something* which one calls conscience made me feel ashamed of the whole matter. I had a feeling of being in the wrong, which is apt to make one vexed and fretful, and it was this, quite as much as fear of my grave father, which made the colour rush to my face, and the tears into my eyes.

"Come, Regie," he said, "out with it. Don't cry, whatever you do; that's like a baby. Have you been doing something wrong? Tell me all about it. Confession is half way to forgiveness. Don't be afraid of me. For heaven's sake, don't be afraid of me!" added my father, with impatient sadness, and the frown deepening so rapidly on his face that my tears flowed in proportion.

(How sad are the helpless struggles of a widowed father with young children, I could not then appreciate. How seldom successful is the alternative of a second marriage, has become proverbial in excess of the truth.)

My father was more patient than many men. He did not dismiss me and my tears to the nursery in despair. With the insight and tenderness of a mother he restrained himself, and unknitting his brows, held out both his hands and said very kindly,

"Come and tell poor Papa all about it, my darling."

On which I jumped from my chair, and rushing up to him, threw my arms about his neck and sobbed out, "Oh, Papa! Papa! I don't want him."

"Don't want *whom*, my boy?"

"M-m-m-m-r. Gray," I sobbed.

"And who on earth is Mr. Gray, Regie?" inquired my perplexed parent.

"The tutor—the new tutor," I explained.

"But *whose* new tutor?" cried the distracted gentleman, whose confusion seemed in no way lessened when I added,

"Mine, Papa; the one you're going to get for me." And as no gleam of intelligence yet brightened his puzzled face, I added, doubtfully, "You are going to get one, aren't you, Papa?"

"What put this idea into your head, Regie?" asked my father, after a pause.

And then I had to explain, feeling very uncomfortable as I did so, how I had overheard a few words at the Rectory, and a few words more at the lodge, and how I had patched my hearsays together and made out that a certain little man was coming to be my tutor, who had previously been tutor somewhere else, and that his name was Gray. And all this time my father did not help me out a bit by word or sign. By the time I had got to the end of my story of what I had heard, and what I had guessed, and what Nurse Bundle and I had made out, I did not need any one to tell me that to listen to what one is not intended to hear is a thing to be ashamed of. My cheeks and ears were very red, and I felt very small indeed.

"Now, Regie," said my father, "I won't say what I think about your listening to Mr. Andrewes and me, in order to find out what I did not choose to tell you. You shall tell me what you think, my boy. Do you think it is a nice thing, a gentlemanly thing, upright, and honest, and worthy of Papa's only son, to sneak about listening to what you were not meant to hear. Now don't begin to cry, Reginald," he added, rather sharply; "you have nothing to cry for, and it's either silly or ill-tempered to whimper because I show you that you've done wrong. Anybody may do wrong; and if you think that you have, why say you're sorry, like a man, and don't do so any more."

I made a strong effort to restrain my tears of shame and vexation, and said very heartily—

"I'm very sorry, Papa. I didn't think of it's being wrong."

"I quite believe that, my boy. But you see that it's not right now, don't you?"

"Oh yes!" I exclaimed, "and I won't listen any more, father." We made it up lovingly, Rubens flying frantically at our heads to join in the kisses and reconciliation. He had been anxiously watching us, being well aware that something was amiss.

"I don't mean to tell you what Mr. Andrewes and I *were*

talking about," said my father, "because I did not wish you to hear. But I will tell you that you made a very bad guess at the secret. We were not talking of a tutor, or dreaming of one, and you have vexed yourself for nothing. However, I think it serves you right for listening. But we won't talk of that any more."

I do not think Nurse Bundle was disposed to blame me as much as I now blamed myself; but she was invariably loyal to my father's decisions, and never magnified her own indulgence in the nursery by pitying me if I got into scrapes in the drawing-room.

"My dear," said she, "your Pa's a gentleman, every inch of him. You listen to him, and try and do as he does, and you'll grow up just such another, and be a pride and blessing to all about you."

But we both rejoiced that at any rate our fears were unfounded in reference to the much-dreaded Mr. Gray.

# CHAPTER XVI

## THE REAL MR. GRAY—NURSE BUNDLE REGARDS HIM WITH DISFAVOUR

My feelings may therefore be "better imagined than described" when, at about ten o'clock the following morning, my father called me downstairs, and said, with an odd expression on his face,

"Regie, Mr. Gray has come."

Not for one instant did I in my mind accuse my father of deceiving me. My faith in him was as implicit as he well deserved that it should be. Black might be white, two and two might make five, impossible things might be possible, but my father could not be in the wrong. It was evident that I must have misunderstood him last night. I looked very crestfallen indeed.

My father, however, seemed particularly cheerful, even inclined to laugh, I thought. He took my hand and we went to the front door, my heart beating wildly, for I was a delicate unrobust lad yet, far too easily upset and excited. More like a girl, in fact, if the comparison be not an insult to such sturdy maids as Cousin Polly.

Juliana Horatia Ewing

Outside we found a man-servant on a bay horse, holding a little white pony, on which, I supposed, the little tutor had been riding. But he himself was not to be seen. I tried hard to be manly and calm, and being much struck by the appearance of the pony, who, when I came down the steps, had turned towards me the gentlest and most intelligent of faces, with a splendid long curly white forelock streaming down between his kind dark eyes, I asked—

"Is that Mr. Gray's pony, father?"

"What do you think of it?" said my father.

"Oh, it's a little dear," was my emphatic answer, and as the pony unmistakably turned his head to me, I met his friendly advances by going up to him, and in another moment my arms were round his neck, and he was rubbing his soft, strong nose against my shoulder, and we were kissing and fondling each other in happy forgetfulness of everything but our sudden friendship, whilst the man-servant (apparently an Irishman) was firing off ejaculations like crackers on the fifth of November.

"Sure, now, did ever anyone see the like—just to look at the baste—sure he knows it's the young squire himself entirely. Och, but the young gintleman's as well acquainted with horses as myself—sure he'd make friends with a unicorn, if there was such an animal; and it's the unicorn that would be proud to let him, too!"

"It has been used to boys, I think?" said my father.

"Ye may say that, yer honour. It likes boys better than man, woman, or child, and it's not every baste ye can say that for."

"A good many beasts have reason to think very differently, I fear," said my father.

"And *that's* as true a word as your honour ever spoke," assented the groom.

Meanwhile a possible ground of consolation was beginning to suggest itself to my mind.

"Will Mr. Gray keep his pony here?" I asked,

"The pony will live here," said my father.

"Oh, do you think," I asked, "do you think, that if I am very good, and do my lessons well, Mr. Gray will sometimes let me ride him? He *is* such a darling!" By which I meant the pony, and not Mr. Gray. My father laughed, and put his hand on my shoulders.

"I have only been teasing you, Regie," he said. "You know I told you there was no tutor in the case. Mr. Andrewes and I were talking about this pony, and when Mr. Andrewes said *grey*, he spoke of the colour of the pony, and not of anybody's name."

"Then is the pony yours?" I asked.

My father looked at my eager face with a pleased smile.

"No, my boy," he said, "he is yours."

The wild delight with which I received this announcement, the way I jumped and danced, and that Rubens jumped and danced with me, my gratitude and my father's satisfaction, the renewed amenities between myself and my pony, his obvious knowledge of the fact that I was his master, and the running commentary of the Irishman, I will not attempt to describe.

Juliana Horatia Ewing

The purchase of this pony was indeed one of my father's many kind thoughts for my welfare and amusement. My odd pilgrimage to the Rectory in search of change and society, and the pettish complaints of dulness and monotony at home which I had urged to account for my freak of "dropping in," had seemed to him not without a certain serious foundation. Except for walks about the farm with him, and stolen snatches of intercourse with the grooms, and dogs, and horses in the stables (which both he and Nurse Bundle discouraged), I had little or no amusement proper to a boy of my age. I was very well content to sit with Rubens at Mrs. Bundle's apron-string, but now and then I was, to use an expressive word, *moped*. My father had taken counsel with Mr. Andrewes, and the end of it all was that I found myself the master of the most charming of ponies, with the exciting prospect before me of learning to ride. The very thought of it invigorated me. Before the Irish groom went away I had asked if my new steed "could jump." I questioned my father's men as to the earliest age at which young gentlemen had ever been allowed to go out hunting, within their knowledge. I went to bed to dream of rides as wild as Mazeppa's, of hairbreadth escapes, and of feats of horsemanship that would have amazed Mr. Astley. And hopes and schemes so wild that I dared not bring them to the test of my father's ridicule, I poured with pride into Nurse Bundle's sympathetic ear.

Dear, good, kind Nurse Bundle! She was indeed a mother to me, and a mother's anxieties and disappointments were her portion. The effect of her watchful constant care of my early years for me, was whatever good there was about me in health or manners. The effect of it for her was, I believe, that she was never thoroughly happy when I was out of her sight. In these circumstances, it seemed hard that when most of my infantile diseases were over, when I was just becoming very intelligent (the best company possible, Mrs. Bundle declared), when I wore my clothes out reasonably, and had exchanged the cries which exercise one's lungs in infancy for rational conversation by the nursery fireside, I should be drawn away from nurse and nursery almost entirely. It was right and natural, but it was hard. Nurse Bundle felt it so, but she never complained. When she felt it most, she only said, "It's all just as it should be." And so it was. Boys and ducklings must wander off some time, be mothers and hens never so kind! The world is wide, and duck-ponds are deep. The young ones must go alone, and those who tremble most for their safety cannot follow to take care of them.

I really shrink from realizing to myself what Nurse Bundle must have suffered whilst I was learning to ride. The novel exercise, the stimulus of risk, that "put new life into me," were to her so many daily grounds for the sad probability of my death.

"Every blessed afternoon do I look to see him brought home on a shutter, with his precious neck broken, poor lamb!" she exclaimed one afternoon, overpowered by the sight of me climbing on to the pony's back, which performance I had brought her downstairs to witness, and endeavoured to render more entertaining and creditable by secretly stimulating the pony to restlessness, and then hopping after him with one foot in the stirrup, in what I fancied to be a very knowing manner.

"Why, my dear Mrs. Bundle," said my father, smiling, "you kill him at least three hundred and sixty-four times oftener in the course of the year than you need. If he does break his neck, he can only do it once, and you bewail his loss every day."

"Now, Heaven bless the young gentleman, sir, and meaning no disrespect, but don't ye go for to tempt Providence by joking about it, and him perhaps brought a hopeless corpse to the side door this very evening," said Mrs. Bundle, her red cheeks absolutely blanched by the vision she had conjured up. Why, I cannot say, but she had fully made up her mind that when I was brought home dead, as she believed that, sooner or later, I was pretty sure to be, I should be brought to the side-door. Now "the side-door," as it was called, was a little door leading into the garden, and less used, perhaps, than any other door in the house. Mrs. Bundle, I believe, had decided that in that tragedy which she was constantly rehearsing, the men who should find my body would avoid the front-door, to spare my father the sudden shock of meeting my corpse. The side-door, too, was just below the nursery windows. Mrs. Bundle herself, would, probably, be the first to hear any knocking at it, and she naturally pictured herself as taking a prominent part in the terrible scene she so often fancied. It was perhaps a good thing, on the whole, that she chose this door in preference to those in constant use, otherwise every ring or knock at the front or back door must have added greatly to her anxieties.

I fear I did not do much to relieve them. I rather aggravated them. Partly I believe in the conceit of showing off my own skill and daring, and partly by way of "hardening" Mrs. Bundle's nerves. When more knowledge, or longer custom, or stronger health or nerves, have placed us beyond certain terrors which afflict other people, we are apt to fancy that, by insisting upon their submitting to what we do not mind, our nervous friends can or ought to be forced into the unconcern which we feel ourselves; which is, perhaps, a little too like dosing the patient with what happens to agree with the doctor.

Thus I fondled my pony's head and dawdled ostentatiously at his heels when Nurse Bundle was most full of fears of his biting or kicking. But I feel sure that this, and the tricks I played to show the firmness of my "seat," only made it seem to her the more certain that, from my recklessness, I must some day be bitten, kicked, or thrown.

I had several falls, and one or two narrow escapes from more serious accidents, which, for the moment, made my father as white as Mrs. Bundle. But he was wise enough to know that the present risks I ran from fearlessness were nothing to the future risks against which complete confidence on horseback would ensure me. And so with the ordinary mishaps, and with days and hours of unspeakable and healthy happiness, I learnt to ride well and to know horses. And poor Mrs. Bundle, sitting safely at home in her rocking-chair, endured all the fears from which I was free.

"Now look, my deary," said she one day; "don't you go turning your sweet face round to look up at the nursery windows when you're a riding off. I can see your curls, bless them! and that's enough for me. Keep yourself still, love, and look where you're a going, for in all reason you've plenty to do with that. And don't you go a waving your precious hand, for it gives me such a turn to think you've let go, and have only got one hand to hold on with, and just turning the corner too, and the pony a shaking its tail, and shifting about with its back legs, till how you don't slip off on one side passes me altogether."

"Why, you don't think I hold on by my hands, do you?" I cried.

"And what should you hold on with?" said Mrs. Bundle. "Many's the light cart I've rode in, but never let go my hold, unless with one hand, to save a bag or a bandbox. And though it's jolting, I'm sure a light cart's nothing to pony-back for starts and unexpectedness."

I tried in vain to make Nurse Bundle like my pony.

"I've seen plenty of ponies!" she said, severely; by which she meant not that she had seen many, but that what she had seen of them had been more than enough. "My brother-in-law's first cousin had one—a little red-haired beast—as vicious as any wild cat. It won a many races, but it was the death of him at last, according to the expectations of everybody. He was brought home on a shutter to his family, and the pony grazing close by in the ditch as if nothing had happened. Many's the time I've seen him on it expecting death as little as yourself, and he refused twenty pound for it the Tuesday fortnight before he was killed. But I was with his wife that's now his widow when the body was brought."

By the time that I heard this anecdote I was happily too good a rider to be frightened by it; but I did wish that Mrs. Bundle's relative had died any other death than that which formed so melancholy a precedent in her mind.

The strongest obstacle, however, to any chance of my nurse's looking with favour on my new pet was her profound ignorance of horses and ponies in general. Except as to colour or length of tail, she recognized no difference between one and another. As to any distinctions between "play" and "vice," a fidgety animal and a determined kicker, a friendly nose-rub and a malicious resolve to bite, they were not discernible by Mrs. Bundle's unaccustomed eyes.

"I've seen plenty of ponies," she would repeat; "I know what they are, my dear," and she invariably followed up this statement by rehearsing the fate of her brother-in-law's cousin, sometimes adding—

"He was very much giving to racing, and being about horses. He was a little man, and suffered a deal from the quinsies in the autumn."

"What a pity he didn't die of a quinsy instead of breaking his neck!" I felt compelled to say one day.

"He might have lived to have done that if it hadn't a been for the pony," said Mrs. Bundle emphatically.

# CHAPTER XVII

## I FAIL TO TEACH LATIN TO MRS. BUNDLE—THE RECTOR TEACHES ME

I was soon to discover the whole of my father's plans with Mr. Andrewes for my benefit. Not only had they decided that I was to have a pony, and learn to ride, but it was also settled that I was to go daily to the Rectory to "do lessons" with the Rector.

I was greatly pleased. I had already begun Latin with my father, and had vainly endeavoured to share my educational advantages with Mrs. Bundle, by teaching her the first declension.

"Musa, amuse," she repeated after me on this occasion.

"Musae, of a muse," I continued.

"*Of amuse!* There's no sense in that, my dearie," said Mrs. Bundle; and as my ideas were not very well defined on the subject of the muses, and as Mrs. Bundle's were even less so as to genders, numbers, and cases, I reluctantly gave in to her decision that "Latin was very well for young gentlemen, but good plain English was best suited to the likes of her."

She was greatly delighted, however, with a Latin valentine which I prepared for her on the ensuing 14th of February, and caused to be delivered by the housemaid, in an envelope with an old stamp, and postmarks made with a pen and a penny. The design was very simple; a heart traced in outline from a peppermint lozenge of that shape, which came to me in an ounce of "mixed sweets" from the village shop. The said heart was painted red and below it I wrote in my largest and clearest handwriting, *Mrs. B. Amo te*. When the Latin was translated for her, her gratification was great. At first she was put out by there being only two Latin words to three English ones, but she got over the difficulty at last by always reading it thus:—

> "A mo te,
> I love thee."

My Latin had not advanced much beyond this stage when I began to go to Mr. Andrewes every day.

Thenceforward I progressed rapidly in my learning. Mr. Andrewes was a good scholar, and (quite another matter) a good teacher; and I fancy that I was not wanting in quickness or in willingness to work. But Latin, and arithmetic, and geography, and the marvellous improvement he soon made in my handwriting, were small parts indeed of all that I owe to that good friend of my childhood. I suppose that—other things being equal—children learn most from those who love them best, and I soon found out that I was the object of a strangely strong affection in my new teacher. The chief cause of this I did not then know, and only learnt when death had put an end, for this life, to our happy intercourse. But I had a child's complacent appreciation of the fact that I was a favourite, and on the strength of it I haunted the Rectory at all hours, confident of a welcome. I turned over the Rector's books, and culled his flowers, and joined his rides, and made him tell me stories, and tyrannized over him as over a docile playfellow in a fashion that astonished many grown-up people who were awed and repelled by his reserve and eccentricities, and who never knew his character as I knew it till he could be known no more. But I fancy that there are not a few worthy men who, shy and reserved, are only intimately known by the children whom they love.

I may say that not only did I owe much more than mere learning to Mr. Andrewes, but that my regular lessons were a small part even of his teaching.

"It always seems to me," he said one day, when my father and I were together at the Rectory, "that there are two kinds of learning more neglected than they should be in the education of the young. Religious knowledge, which, after all, concerns the worthiest part of every man, and the longest share of his existence (to say nothing of what it has to do with matters now); and the knowledge of what we call Nature, and of all the laws which concern our bodies, and rule the conditions of life in this world. It's a hobby of mine, Mr. Dacre, and I'm afraid I ride my hobbies rather like a witch on a broomstick. But a man must deal according to his lights and his conscience; and if I am intrusted with the lad's education for a while, it will be my duty and pleasure to instruct him in religious lore and natural science, so far as his age allows. To teach him to know his Bible (and I wish all who have the leisure were taught to read the Scriptures in the original tongues). To teach him to know his Prayer-book, and its history. Something, too, of the history of his Church, and of the faith in which better men than us have been proud to live, and for which some have even dared to die."

When the Rector became warm in conversation, his voice betrayed a rougher accent than we commonly heard, and the more excited he became the broader was his speech. It had got very broad at this point, when my father broke in. "I trust him entirely to you, sir," he said; "but, pardon me, I confess I am not fond of religious prodigies—children who quote texts and teach their elders their duty; and Reginald has quite sufficient tendency towards over-excitement of brain on all subjects."

"I quite agree with you," said Mr. Andrewes. "I think you may trust me. I know well that childhood, like all states and times of ignorance, is so liable to conceit and egotism, that to foster religious self-importance is only too easy, and modesty and moderation are more slowly taught. But if youth is a time when one is specially apt to be self-conceited, surely, Mr. Dacre, it is also the first, the easiest, the purest, and the most zealous in which to learn what is so seldom learned in good time."

"I dare say you are right," said my father.

"People talk with horror of attacks on the faith as sadly characteristic of our age," said the Rector, walking up and down the study, and seemingly forgetful of my presence, if not of my father's, "(which, by-the-bye, is said of every age in turn), but I fear the real evil is that so few have any fixed faith to be attacked. It is the old, old story. From within, not from without. The armour that was early put on, that has grown with our growth, that has been a strength in time of trial, and a support in sorrow, and has given grace to joy, will not quickly be discarded because the journals say it is old-fashioned and worn-out. Life is too short for every man to prove his faith theoretically, but it is given to all to prove its practical value by experience, and that method of proof cannot be begun too soon."

"Very true," said my father.

Juliana Horatia Ewing

"I don't know why a man's religious belief (which is of course the ground of his religious life) should be supposed to come to him without the trouble of learning, any more than any other body of truths and principles on which people act," Mr. Andrewes went on. "And yet what religious instruction do young people of the educated classes receive as a rule?— especially the boys, for girls get hold of books, and pick up a faith somehow, though often only enough to make them miserable and 'unsettled,' and no more. I often wonder," he added, sitting down at the table with a laugh, "whether the mass of educated men know less of what concerns the welfare of their souls, and all therewith connected, or the mass of educated women of what concerns their bodies, and all *therewith* connected. I feel sure that both ignorances produce untold and dire evil!"

"So theology and natural science are to be Regie's first lessons?" said my father, drawing me to him.

"I've been talking on stilts, I know," said Mr. Andrewes, smiling. "We'll use simpler terms,—duty to GOD, and duty to Man. One can't do either without learning how, Mr. Dacre."

I repeat this conversation as I have heard it from my father, since I grew up and could understand it. Mr. Andrewes' educational theories were duly put in practice for my benefit. In his efforts for my religious education, Nurse Bundle proved an unexpected ally. When I repeated to her some solemn truth which in his reverent and simple manner he had explained to me; some tale he had told me of some good man, whose example was to be followed; some bit of quaint practical advice he had given me, or perhaps some hymn I had learned by his side, the delight of the good old soul knew no bounds. She said it was as good as a sermon; and as she was particularly fond of sermons, this was a compliment.

She used to beg me carefully to remember anything of the kind that I heard, and when I repeated it, she had generally her own word of advice to add, and wonderful tales with which to point the moral,—tales of happy and unhappy deathbeds, of warnings, judgments, and answers to prayer. Tales, too, of the charities of the poor, the happiness of the afflicted, and the triumphs of the deeply tempted, such as it is good for the wealthy, and healthy, and well-cared-for, to listen to. Nurse Bundle's religious faith had a tinge of superstition; that of Mr. Andrewes was more enlightened. But with both it was a matter of every-day life, from which no hope or fear, no sorrow or joy, no plan, no word or deed, could be separated.

And however imperfectly, so it became with me. Like most children, I had my own rather vivid idea of the day of judgment. The thought of death was familiar to me. (It is seldom, I think, a painful one in childhood.) I fully realized the couplet which concluded a certain quaint old rhyme in honour of the four Evangelists which Nurse Bundle had taught me to repeat in bed—

"If I die before I wake,
I pray the Lord my soul to take."

I used to recite a similar one when I was dressed in the morning—

"If my soul depart to-day,
A place in Paradise I pray."

When I had had a particularly pleasant ride, or enjoyed myself much during the day, I thanked GOD specially in my evening prayers. I remember that whatever I wished for I prayed for, in the complete belief that this was the readiest way to obtain it. And it would be untruth to my childish experience not to add that I never remember to have prayed in vain. I also picked up certain little quaint superstitions from Nurse Bundle, some of which cling to me still. Neither she nor I ever put anything on the top of a Bible, and we sometimes sat long in comical and uncomfortable silence because neither of us would "scare the angel that was passing over the house." When the first notes of the organ stirred the swallows in the church eaves to chirp aloud, I believed with Mrs. Bundle that they were joining in the Te Deum. And when sunshine fell on me through the church windows during service, I regarded it as "a blessing."

The other half of Mr. Andrewes' plan was not neglected. From him I learnt (and it is lore to be thankful for) to use my eyes. He was a good botanist, and his knowledge of the medicinal uses of wild herbs ranked next to his piety to raise him in Mrs. Bundle's esteem. When "lessons" were over, we often rode out together. As we rode through the lanes, he taught me to distinguish the notes of the birds, to observe what crops grow on certain soils, and at what seasons the different plants flower and bear fruit. He made me see with my own eyes, and hear with my own ears, for which I shall ever be grateful to him. I fancy I can hear his voice now, saying in his curt cutting fashion—

"How silly it sounds to hear anybody with a head on his shoulders say, 'I never noticed it!' What are eyes for?"

If I admired some creeper-covered cottage, picturesquely old and tumble-down, he would ask me how many rooms I thought it contained—if I fancied the roof would keep out rain or snow, and how far I supposed it was convenient and comfortable for a man and his wife and six children to live in. In some very practical problems which he once set me, I had to suppose myself a labourer, with nine shillings a week, and having found out what sum that would come to in half a year, to write on my slate how I would spend the money, to the best advantage, in clothing and feeding two grown-up people and seven children of various ages. As I knew nothing of the cost of the necessaries of life, I went, by Mr. Andrewes' advice, to Nurse Bundle for help.

"What do beef and mutton cost?" was my first question, as I sat with an important air at the nursery table, slate in hand.

"Now bless the dear boy's innocence?" cried Mrs. Bundle. "You may leave the beef and mutton, love. It's not much meat a family gets that's reared on nine shillings a week."

After a series of calculations for oatmeal-porridge, onion-potage, and other modest dainties, during which Mrs. Bundle constantly fell back on the "bits of things in the garden," I said decidedly—

"They can't have any clothes, so it's no good thinking about it."

"Children can't be let go bare-backed," said Mrs. Bundle, with equal decision. "She must take in washing. For in all reason, boots can't be expected to come out of nine shillings a week, and as many mouths to feed."

"She must take in washing, sir," I announced with a resigned air, and the old-fashioned gravity peculiar to me, when I returned to the Rectory next day. "Boots can't come out of nine shillings a week."

The Rector smiled.

"And suppose one of the boys catches a fever, as you did; and they can't have other people's clothes to the house, because of the infection. And then there will be the doctor's bill to pay—what then?"

By this time I had so thoroughly realized the position of the needy family, that I had forgotten it was not a real case, or rather, that no special one was meant. And I begged, with tears in my eyes, that I might apply the contents of my alms-box to paying the doctor's bill.

Many a lesson like this, with oft-repeated practical remarks about healthy situations, proper drainage, roomy cottages, and the like, was engraven by constant repetition on my mind, and bore fruit in after years, when the welfare of many labourers and their families was in my hands.

It is difficult to convey an idea of the learning I gained from my good friend, and yet to show how free he was from priggishness, or from always playing the schoolmaster. He was simply the most charming of companions, who tried to raise me to his level, and interest me in what he knew and thought himself, instead of coming down to me, and talking the patronizing nonsense which is so often supposed to be acceptable to children.

Across all the years that have parted us in this life I fancy at times that I see his grey eyes twinkling under their thick brows once more, and hear his voice, with its slightly rough accent, saying—

"*Think*, my dear lad, *think*! Pray learn to think!"

# CHAPTER XVIII

## THE ASTHMATIC OLD GENTLEMAN AND HIS RIDDLES—I PLAY TRUANT AGAIN—IN THE BIG GARDEN

It was perhaps partly because, like most only children, I was accustomed to be with grown-up people, that I liked the way in which Mr. Andrewes treated me, and resented the very different style of another friend of my father, who always bantered me in a playful, nonsensical fashion, which he deemed suitable to my years.

The friend in question was an old gentleman, and a very benevolent one. I think he was fond of children, and I am sure he was kind.

He never came without giving me half-a-guinea before he left, generally slipping it down the back of my neck, or hiding it under my plate at dinner, or burying it in an orange. He had a whole store of funny tricks, which would have amused and pleased me if I might have enjoyed them in peace. But he never ceased teasing me, and playing practical jokes on me. And the worst of it was, he teased Rubens also.

Mr. Andrewes often afterwards told of the day when I walked into the Rectory—my indignant air, he vowed, faithfully copied by the dog at my heels, and without preface began:

"I know I ought to forgive them that trespass against us, but I can't. He put cayenne pepper on to Rubens' nose."

In justice to ourselves, I must say that neither Rubens nor I bore malice on this point, but it added to the anxiety which I always felt to get out of the old gentleman's way.

By him I was put through those riddles which puzzle all childish brains in turn: "If a herring and a half cost threehalfpence," etc. And if I successfully accomplished this calculation, I was tripped up by the unfair problem, "If your grate is of such and such dimensions, what will the coals come to?" I can hear his voice now (hoarse from a combination of asthma and snuff-taking) as he poked me jocosely but unmercifully "under the fifth rib," as he called it, crying—

"*Ashes*! my little man. D'ye see? *Ashes*! *Ashes*!"

After which he took more snuff, and nearly choked himself with laughing at my chagrin.

Greatly was Nurse Bundle puzzled that night, when I stood, ready for bed, fumbling with both hands under my nightshirt, and an expression of face becoming a surgeon conducting a capital operation.

"Bless the dear boy!" she cried. "What are you doing to yourself, my dear?"

"How does he *know* which is the fifth rib?" I almost howled in my vexation. "I don't believe it *was* the fifth rib! I wish I *hadn't* a fifth rib! I wish I might hurt *his* fifth rib!"

I think the old gentleman would have choked with laughter if he could have seen and heard me.

One day, to my father's horror, I candidly remarked,

"It always makes me think of the first of April, sir, when you're here."

I did not mean to be rude. It was simply true that the succession of "sells" and practical jokes of which Rubens and I were the victims during his visits did recall the tricks supposed to be sacred to the Festival of All Fools.

To do the old gentleman justice, he heartily enjoyed the joke at his own expense; laughed and took snuff in extra proportions, and gave me a whole guinea instead of half a one, saying that I should go to live with him in Fools' Paradise, where little pigs ran about ready roasted with knives and forks in their backs; adding more banter and nonsense of the same kind, to the utter bewilderment of my brain.

He was the occasion of my playing truant to the Rectory a second time. Once, when he was expected, I took my nightshirt from my pillow, and followed by Rubens, presented myself before the Rector as he sat at breakfast, saying, "Mr. Carpenter is coming, and we can't endure it. We really can't endure it. And please, sir, can you give us a bed for the night? And I'm very sorry it isn't a clean one, but Nurse keeps the nightgowns on the top shelf, and I didn't want her to know we were coming."

Mr. Andrewes kept me with him for some hours, but he persuaded me to return and meet the old gentleman, saying that it was only due to his real kindness to bear with his little jokes; and that I ought to try and learn to make allowances, and "put up with" things that were not quite to my mind. So I went back, and partly because of my efforts to be less easily annoyed, and partly because I was older than at his latest visit, and knew all the riddles, and could see through his jokes more quickly, I got on very well with him.

Very glad I was afterwards that I had gone back and spent a friendly evening with the kind old man; for the following spring his asthma became worse and worse, and he died. That visit was his last to us. He teased me and Rubens no more. But when I heard of his death, I felt what I said, that I was very sorry. He had been very kind and his pokes and jokes were trifles to look back upon.

Mr. Andrewes kept up his interest in my garden. Indeed, I soon got beyond the childish way of gardening; I ceased to use my watering-pot recklessly, and to take up my plants to see how they were getting on. I was promoted from my little beds to some share in the large flower-garden. My father was very fond of his flowers, and greatly pleased to find me useful.

Some of the happiest hours I ever spent were those in which I worked with him in "the big garden;" Rubens lying in the sun, keeping imaginary guard over my father's coat. We had a friendly rivalry with the Rectory, in which I felt the highest interest. Sometimes, however, I helped Mr. Andrewes himself, when he rewarded me with plants and good advice. The latter often in quaint rhymes, such as

"This rule in gardening never forget,
To sow dry, and to set wet."

But after a time, and to my deep regret, Mr. Andrewes gave up the care of my education. He said his duties in the parish did not allow of his giving much time to me; and though my father had no special wish to press my studies, and was more anxious for the benefit of the Rector's influence, Mr. Andrewes at last persuaded him that he ought to get a resident tutor and prepare me for a public school.

By this time I had almost forgotten my foolish prejudice against the imaginary Mr. Gray, and was only sorry that I could no longer do lessons with the Rector.

I suppose it was in answer to some inquiries that he made that my father heard of a gentleman who wanted such a situation as ours. He heard of him from Leo Damer's guardian, and the gentleman proved to be the very tutor whom I had seen from the nursery windows of Aunt Maria's house. He had remained with Leo ever since, but as Leo's guardian had now sent him to school, the tutor was at liberty.

In these circumstances, I felt that he was not quite a stranger, and was prepared to receive him favourably.

Indeed, when his arrival was close at hand, Nurse Bundle and I took an hospitable pleasure in looking over the arrangements of his room, and planning little details for his comfort.

He came at last, and my father was able to announce to Aunt Maria (who had never approved of what she called "Mr. Andrewes' desultory style of teaching") that my education was now placed in the hands of a resident tutor.

Juliana Horatia Ewing

# CHAPTER XIX

## THE TUTOR—THE PARISH—A NEW CONTRIBUTOR TO THE ALMS-BOX

Mr. Clerke was a small, slight, fair man. He was short-sighted, which caused him to carry a round piece of glass about the size of a penny in his waistcoat pocket, and from time to time to stick this into his eye, where he held it in a very ingenious, but, as it seemed to me, dangerous fashion.

It took me quite a fortnight to get used to that eye-glass. It was like a policeman's bull's-eye lantern. I never knew when it might be turned on me. Then the glass had no rim, the edges looked quite sharp, and the reckless way in which the tutor held it squeezed between his cheek and eyebrow was a thing to be at once feared and admired.

I was sitting over my Delectus one morning, unwillingly working at a page which had been set as a punishment for some offence, with my hands buried in my pockets, fumbling with halfpence and other treasures there concealed, when, seeing my tutor stick his glass into his eye as he went to the bookcase, I pulled out a halfpenny to try if I could hold it between cheek and brow, as he held his glass. After many failures, I had just triumphantly succeeded when he caught sight of my reflection in a mirror, and seeing the halfpenny in my eye, my chin in air, and my face puckered up with what must have been a comical travesty of his own appearance, he concluded that I was mimicking him, and defying his authority, and coming quickly up to me he gave me a sharp box on the ear.

In the explanation which followed, he was candid enough to apologize handsomely for having "lost his temper," as he said; and having remitted my task as an atonement, took me out fishing with him.

We got on very well together. At first I think my old-fashioned ways puzzled him, and he was also disconcerted by the questions which I asked when we were out together. Perhaps he understood me better when he came to know Mr. Andrewes, and learned how much I had been with him.

He had a very high respect for the Rector. The first walk we took together was to call at the Rectory. We stayed luncheon, and Mr. Andrewes had some conversation with the tutor which I did not hear. As we came home, I was anxious to learn if Mr. Clerke did not think my dear friend "very nice."

"Mr. Andrewes is a very remarkable man," said the tutor. And he constantly repeated this. "He is a very remarkable man."

After a while Mr. Clerke ceased to be put out by my asking strange unchildish questions which he was not always able to answer. He often said, "We will ask Mr. Andrewes what he thinks;" and for my own part, I respected him none the less that he often honestly confessed that he could not, off-hand, solve all the problems that exercised my brain. He was not a good general naturalist but he was fond of geology, and was kind enough to take me out with him on "chipping" expeditions, and to start me with a "collection" of fossils. I had already a collection of flowers, a collection of shells, a collection of wafers, and a collection of seals. (People did not collect monograms and old stamps in my young days.) These collections were a sore vexation to Nurse Bundle.

"Whatever a gentleman like the Rector is thinking of, for to encourage you in such rubbish, my dear," said she, "it passes me! It's vexing enough to see dirt and bits about that shouldn't be, when you can take the dust-pan and clear 'em away. But to have dead leaves, and weeds, and stones off the road brought in day after day, and not be allowed so much as to touch them, and a young gentleman that has things worth golden guineas to play with, storing up a lot of stuff you could pick off any rubbish-heap in a field before it's burned—if it was anybody but you, my dear, I couldn't abear it. And what's a tutor for, I should like to know?"

(Mrs. Bundle, who at no time liked blaming her darling, had now acquired a habit of laying the blame of any misdoings of mine on the tutor, on the ground that he "ought to have seen to" my acting differently.)

If Mr. Clerke discovered that he could confess to being puzzled by some of my questions, without losing ground in his pupil's respect, I soon found out that my grown-up tutor had not altogether outlived boyish feelings. It dimly dawned on me that he liked a holiday quite as well, if not better than myself; and as we grew more intimate we had many a race and scramble and game together, when bookwork was over for the day. He rode badly, but with courage, and the mishaps he managed to suffer when riding the quietest and oldest of my father's horses were food for fun with him as well as with me.

He told me that he was going to be a clergyman, and on Sunday afternoons we commonly engaged in strong religious discussions. During the fruit season it was also our custom on that day to visit the kitchen-garden after luncheon, where we ate gooseberries, and settled our theological differences. There is a little low, hot stone seat by one of the cucumber frames on which I never can seat myself now without recollections of the flavour of the little round, hairy, red gooseberries, and of a lengthy dispute which I held there with Mr. Clerke, and which began by my saying that I looked forward to meeting Rubens "in a better world." I distinctly remember that I could bring forward so little authority for my belief, and the tutor so little against it, that we adjourned by common consent to the Rectory to take Mr. Andrewes' opinion, and taste his strawberries.

I feel quite sure that Mr. Clerke, as well as myself, strongly felt the Rector's influence. He often said in after-years how much he owed to him for raising his aims and views about the sacred office which he purposed to fill. He had looked forward to being a clergyman as to a profession towards which his education and college career had tended, and which, he hoped, would at last secure him a comfortable livelihood through the interest of some of his patrons. But intercourse with the Rector gave a higher tone to his ideas. He would have been a clergyman of high character otherwise, but now he aimed at holiness; he would never have been an idle one, but now his wish was to learn how much he could do, and how well he could do that much for the people who should be committed to his charge. He was by no means a reticent man, he liked sympathy, and soon got into the habit of confiding in me for want of a better friend. Thus as he began to take a most earnest interest in parish work, and in schemes for the benefit of the people, our Sunday conversations became less controversial, and we gossiped about schools and school-treats, cricket-clubs, drunken fathers, slattern mothers, and spoiled children, and how the evening hymn "went" after the sermon on Sunday, like district visitors at a parish tea-party. What visions of improvement amongst our fellow-creatures we saw as we wandered about amongst the gooseberry-bushes, Rubens following at my heels, and eating a double share from the lower branches, since his mouth had not to be emptied for conversation! We often got parted when either of us wandered off towards special and favourite trees. Those bearing long, smooth green gooseberries like grapes, or the highly-ripened yellows, or the hairy little reds. Then we shouted bits of gossip, or happy ideas that struck us, to each other across the garden. And full of youth and hopefulness, in the sunshine of these summer Sundays, we gave ourselves credit for clear-sightedness in all our opinions, and promised ourselves success for every plan, and gratitude from all our proteges.

Mr. Andrewes had started a Sunday School with great success (Sunday Schools were novelties then), and Mr. Clerke was a teacher. At last, to my great delight, I was allowed to take the youngest class, and to teach them their letters and some of the Catechism.

About this time I firmly resolved to be a parson when I grew up. My great practical difficulty on this head was that I must, of course, live at Dacrefield, and yet I could not be the Rector. My final decision I announced to Mr. Andrewes.

"Mr. Clerke and I will always be curates, and work under you."

On which the tutor would sigh, and say, "I wish it could be so, Regie, for I do not think I shall ever like any other place, or church, or people so well again."

At this time my alms-box was well filled, thanks to the liberality of Mr. Clerke. He now taxed his small income as I taxed my pocket-money (a very different matter!), and though I am sure he must sometimes have been inconveniently poor, he never failed to put by his share of our charitable store.

Some brooding over the matter led me to say to him one Sunday, "You and I, sir, are like the widow and the other people in the lesson to-day: I put into the box out of my pocket-money, and you out of your living."

The tutor blushed painfully; partly, I think, at my accurate comprehension of the difference between our worldly lots, and partly in sheer modesty at my realizing the measure of his self-sacrifice.

When first he began to contribute, he always kept back a certain sum, which he as regularly sent away, to whom I never knew. He briefly explained, "It is for a good object." But at last a day came when he announced, "I no longer have that call upon me." And as at the same time he put on a black tie, and looked grave for several days, I judged that some poor relation, who was now dead, had been the object of his kindness. He spoke once more on the subject, when he thanked me for having led him to put by a fixed sum for such purposes, and added, "The person to whom I have been accustomed to send that share of the money said that it was worth double to have it regularly."

# CHAPTER XX

## THE TUTOR'S PROPOSAL—A TEACHERS' MEETING

I think it was Mr. Clerke who first suggested that we should take the Sunday scholars and teachers for a holiday trip. Such things are matters of course now in every parish, but in my childhood it was considered a most marvellous idea by our rustic population. The tutor had heard of some extraordinarily active parson who had done the like by his schools, and partly from real kindness, and partly in the spirit of emulation which intrudes even upon schemes of benevolence, he was most anxious that we at Dacrefield should not "be behindhand" in good works. Competition is a feeling with which children have great sympathy, and I warmly echoed Mr. Clerke's resolve that we would not "be behindhand."

"Let us go to the Rectory at once," said I; "Mr. Andrewes said we might have some of those big yellow raspberries, and we must ask him about it. It's a splendid idea. But where shall we go?"

The matter resolved itself into this question. The Rector was quite willing for the treat. My father gave us a handsome subscription; the farmers followed the Squire's lead. Mr.

Andrewes was not behindhand. The tutor and I considered the object a suitable one for aid from our alms-box. There was no difficulty whatever. Only—where were we to go?

Finally, we all decided that we would go to Oakford.

It was not because Oakford had been the end of our consultation long ago, after my illness, nor because Nurse Bundle had any voice in the matter, it was a certain bullet-headed, slow-tongued old farmer, one of our teachers, who voted for our going to Oakford; and more by persistently repeating his advice than by any very strong reasons there seemed to be for our following it, he carried the day.

"I've know'd Oakford, man and boy, for twenty year," he repeated, at intervals of three minutes or so, during what would now be called a "teachers' meeting" in the school-room. In fact, Oakford was his native place, though he was passing his old age in Dacrefield, and he had a natural desire to see it again, and a natural belief that the spot where he had been young and strong, and light-hearted, had especial merits of its own.

Even though we had nothing better to propose, old Giles' love for home would hardly have decided us, but he had something more to add. There was a "gentleman's place" on the outskirts of Oakford, which sometimes, in the absence of the family, was "shown" to the public: old Giles had seen it as a boy, and the picture he drew of its glories fairly carried us away, the Rector and tutor excepted. They shrugged their shoulders with faces of comical despair as the old man, having fairly taken the lead, babbled on about the "picters," the "stattys," and the "yaller satin cheers" in the grand drawing-room; whilst the other teachers listened with open mouths, and an evident and growing desire to see Oakford Grange. I did not half believe in old Giles' wonders, and yet I wished to see the place myself, if only to learn how much of all he described to us was true. I supposed that "the family" must have been at home when I was at Oakford, or Mr. and Mrs. Buckle would surely have taken me to see the Grange.

The Rector suggested that the family might be at home now, and we might have our expedition for nothing; but it appeared that old Giles' sister's grandson had been over to see his great-uncle only a fortnight ago, "come Tuesday," and had distinctly stated that the family "was in furrin' parts," and would be so for months to come. Moreover, he had said that there was a rumour that the place was to be sold, and nobody knew if the next owner would allow it to be "shown," even in his absence. Thus it was evident that if we wanted to see the Grange, it must be "now or never."

On hearing this, our fattest and richest farmer (he took an upper class in school more in deference to his position than to the rather scanty education which accompanied it) rose and addressed the Rector as follows:—

"Reverend sir. I takes the liberty of rising and addressin' of you, with my respex to yourself and Mr. Clerke, and the young gentleman as represents the Squire I've a-been tenant to, man and boy, this thirty year and am proud to name it." (Murmurs of applause from one or two other farmers present, my father being very popular.)

"Reverend sir. I began with bird-scaring, and not a penny in my pocket, that wouldn't have held coppers for holes, if I had, and clothes that would have scared of themselves, letting alone clappers. The Squire knows how much of his land I have under my hand now, and your reverence is acquainted with the years I've been churchwarden.

"Reverend Sir. I am proud to have rose by my own exertions.

I never iggerantly set *my*self against improvements and opportoonities." (Gloom upon the face of the teacher of the fourth class, who objected to machinery, and disbelieved in artificial manures.) "*My* mottor 'as allus been, 'Never lose a chance;' and that's what I ses on this occasion; 'never lose a chance.'"

As our churchwarden backed his advice by offering to lend waggons and horses to take us to Oakford, if the other farmers would do the same, his speech decided the matter. We all wanted to go to Oakford, and to Oakford it was decided that we should go.

Juliana Horatia Ewing

# CHAPTER XXI

## OAKFORD ONCE MORE—THE SATIN CHAIRS— THE HOUSEKEEPER—THE LITTLE LADIES AGAIN—FAMILY MONUMENTS

The expedition was very successful, and we all returned in safety to Dacrefield; rather, I think, to the astonishment of some of the good-wives of the village, who looked upon any one who passed the parish bounds as a traveller, and thought our jaunt to Oakford "venturesome" almost to a "tempting of Providence."

It is a curious study to observe what things strike different people on occasions of this kind.

It was not the house itself, though the building was remarkably fine (a modern erection on the site of the old "Grange"), nor the natural features of the place, though they were especially beautiful, that roused the admiration of our teachers and their scholars. Somebody said that the house was "a deal bigger than the Hall" (at Dacrefield), and one or two criticisms were passed upon the timber; but the noble park, the grand slopes, the lovely peeps of distance, the exquisite taste displayed in the grounds and gardens about the house, drew little attention from our party. Within, the succession of big rooms became confusing. One or two bits in certain pictures were pronounced by the farmers "as natteral as life;" the "stattys" rather scandalized them, and the historical legends attached by the housekeeper to various pieces of furniture fell upon ears too little educated to be interested. But when we got to the big drawing-room the yellow satin chairs gave general and complete satisfaction. When old Giles said, "Here they be!" we felt that all he had told us before was justified, and that we had not come to Oakford in vain. We stroked them, some of the more adventurous sat upon them, and we echoed the churchwarden's remark, "Yaller satin, sure enough, and the backs gilded like a picter-frame."

I cannot but think that the housekeeper must have had friends visiting her that day, which made our arrival inconvenient and tried her temper—she was so very cross. She ran through a hasty account of each room in injured tones, but she resented questions, refused explanations, and was particularly irritable if anybody strayed from the exact order in which she chose to marshal us through the house. A vein of sarcasm in her remarks quite overpowered our farmers.

"Please to stand off the walls. There ain't no need to crowd up against them in spacyous rooms like these, and the paper ain't one of your cheap ones with a spotty pattern as can be patched or matched anywhere. It come direct from the Indies, and the butterflies and the dragons is as natteral as life. 'Whose picter's that in the last room?' You should have kept with the party, young woman, and then you'd 'ave knowed. Parties who don't keep with the party, and then wants the information repeated, will be considered as another party, and must pay accordingly. Next room, through the white door to the left. Now, sir, we're a-waiting for you! All together, if you please!"

But in spite of the good lady, I generally managed to linger behind, or run before, and so to look at things in my own way. Once, as she was rehearsing the history of a certain picture, I made my way out of the room, and catching sight of some pretty things through an open door at the end of the passage, I went in to see what I could see. Some others were following me when the housekeeper spied them, and bustled up, angrily recalling us, for the room, as we found, was a private *boudoir*, and not one of those shown to the public. In my brief glance, however, I had seen something which made me try to get some information out of the housekeeper, in spite of her displeasure.

"Who are those little girls in the picture by the sofa?" I asked. "Please tell me."

"I gives all information in reference to the public rooms," replied the housekeeper, loftily, "as in duty bound; but the private rooms is not in my instructions."

And nothing more could I get out of her to explain the picture which had so seized upon my fancy.

It was a very pretty painting—a modern one. Just the heads and shoulders of two little girls, one of them having her face just below that of the other, whose little arms were round her sister's neck. I knew them in an instant. There was no mistaking that look of decision in the face of the protecting little damsel, nor the wistful appealing glance in the eyes of the other. The artist had caught both most happily; and though the fair locks I had admired were uncovered, I knew my little ladies of the beaver bonnets again.

Having failed to learn anything about them from the housekeeper, I went to old Giles and asked him the name of the gentleman to whom the place belonged.

"St. John," he replied.

"I suppose he has got children?" I continued.

"Only one living," said old Giles. "They do say he've buried six, most on 'em in galloping consumptions. It do stand to reason they've had all done for 'em that gold could buy, but afflictions, sir, they be as heavy on the rich man as the poor; and when a body's time be come it ain't outlandish oils nor furrin parts can cure 'em."

I wondered which of the quaint little ladies had died, and whether they had taken her to "furrin parts" before her death; and I thought if it were the grey-eyed little maid, how sad and helpless her little sister must be.

"Only one left?" I said mechanically.

"Ay, ay," said old Giles; "and he be pretty bad, I fancy. They've got him in furrin parts where the sun shines all along; but they do say he be wild to get back home, but that'll not be, but in his coffin, to be laid with the rest in the big vault. Ay, ay, affliction spares none, sir, nor yet death."

So this last of the St. John family was a boy. If the little ladies were his sisters, both must be dead; if not, I did not know who they were. I felt very angry with the housekeeper for her sulky reticence. I was also not highly pleased by her manner of treating me, for she evidently took me for one of the Sunday-school boys. I fear it was partly a shabby pride on this point which led me to "tip" her with half-a-crown on my own account when we were taking leave. In a moment she became civil to slavishness, hoped I had enjoyed myself, and professed her willingness to show me anything about the place any day when there were not so "many of them school children crowging and putting a body out, sir. There's such a many common people comes, sir," she added, "I'm quite wored out, and having no need to be in service, and all my friends a-begging of me to leave. I only stays to oblige Mr. St. John."

It was, I think, chiefly in the way I had of thinking aloud that I said, more to myself than to her, "I'm sure I don't know what makes him keep you, you do it so very badly. But perhaps you're respectable."

The half-crown had been unexpected, and this blow fairly took away her breath. Before her rage found words, we were gone.

I did not fail to call on Mr. and Mrs. Buckle. The shop looked just the same as when I was there with Mrs. Bundle. One would have said those were the very rolls of leather that used to stand near the door. The good people were delighted to see me, and proud to be introduced to Mr. Andrewes and my tutor. I had brought some little presents with me, both from myself and Nurse Bundle, which gave great satisfaction.

"And where is Jemima?" I asked, as I sat nursing an imposing-looking parcel addressed to her, which was a large toilette pincushion made and ready furnished with pins for her by Mrs. Bundle herself.

"Now, did you ever!" cried Mrs. Buckle in her old style; "to think of the young gentleman's remembering our Jemima, and she married to Jim Espin the tinsmith this six months past."

So to the tinsmith's I went, and Jemima was, as she expressed it, "that pleased she didn't know where to put herself," by my visit. She presented me with a small tin lantern on which I had made some remark, and which pleased me well. I saw the drawer of farthing wares also, and might have had a flat iron had I been so minded; but I was too old now to want it for a plaything, and too young yet to take it as a remembrance of the past.

I asked Mrs. Buckle about the two little beaver-bonneted ladies, but she did not help me much. She did not remember them. They might be Mr. St. John's little girls; he had buried four. A many ladies wore beaver bonnets then. This was all she could say, so I gave up my inquiries. It was as we were on our way from the Buckles to join the rest of the party that Mr. Clerke caught sight of the quaint little village church, and as churches and church services were matters of great interest to us just then, the two parsons, the churchwarden, five elder scholars and myself got the key from the sexton and went to examine the interior.

It was an old and rather dilapidated building. The glass in the east window was in squares of the tint and consistency of "bottle glass," except where one fragment of what is technically known as "ruby" bore witness that there had once been a stained window there. There were dirty calico blinds to do duty for stained glass in moderating the light; dirt, long gathered, had blunted the sharpness of the tracery on the old carved stalls in the chancel, where the wood-worms of several generations had eaten fresh patterns of their own, and the squat, solemn little carved figures seemed to moulder under one's eyes. In the body of the church were high pews painted white, and four or five old tombs with life-size recumbent figures fitted in oddly with these, and a skimpy looking prayer-desk, pulpit, and font, which were squeezed together between the half-rotten screen and a stone knight in armour.

"Pretty tidy," said our churchwarden, tapping of the pews

with a patronising finger; "but bless and save us, Mr. Andrewes, sir, the walls be disgraceful dirty, and ten shillings' worth of lime and labour would make 'em as white as the driven snow. The sexton says there be a rate, and if so, why don't they whitewash and paint a bit, and get rid of them rotten old seats, and make things a bit decent? You don't find a many places to beat Dacrefield, sir, go as far as you will," he added complacently, and with an air of having exhausted experience in the matter of country churches.

"Them old figures," he went on, "they puts me in mind of one my father used to tell us about, that was in Dacrefield Church. A man with a kind of cap on his face, and his feet crossed, and very pointed toes, and a sword by his side."

"At Dacrefield?" cried Mr. Andrewes; "surely there isn't a Templar at Dacrefield?"

"It were in the old church that came down," continued the churchwarden, "in the old Squire's time. There was a deal of ancient rubbish cleared out then, sir, I've heard, and laid in the stackyard at the Hall. It were when my father were employed as mason under 'brick and mortar Benson,' as they called him, for repairs of a wall, and they were short of stones, and they chipped up the figure I be telling you of. My father allus said he knowed the head was put in whole, and many's the time I've looked for it when a boy."

I think Mr. Andrewes could endure the churchwarden's tale of former destructiveness no longer, and he abruptly called us to come away. I was just running to join the rest at the door, when my eye fell upon a modern tablet of marble above a large cushioned pew. Like the other monuments in the church, it was sacred to the memory of members of the St. John family, and, as I found recorded the names of the wife and six children of the present owner of the estate. Very pathetic, after the record of such desolation, were the words of Job (cut below the bas-relief at the bottom, which, not very gracefully, represented a broken flower): "The LORD gave, and the LORD hath taken away: blessed be the name of the LORD."

Mr. Clerke was hurrying back up the church to fetch me as I read the text. I had just time to see that the last two names were the names of girls, before I had to join him.

Amy and Lucy. Were those indeed the dainty little children who such a short time ago were living, and busy like myself, happy with the tinsmith's toys, and sad for a drenched doll? Wild speculations floated through my head as I followed the tutor, without hearing one word of what he was saying about tea and teachers, and reaching Dacrefield before dark.

I had wished to be their brother. Supposing it had been so, and that I were now withering under the family doom, homesick and sick unto death "in furrin parts!" My last supposition I thought aloud:

"I suppose they know all the old knights, and those people in ruffs, with their sons and daughters kneeling behind them, now. That is, if they were good, and went to heaven."

"*Who* do you suppose know the people in the ruffs?" asked the bewildered tutor.

"Amy and Lucy St. John," said I; "the children who died last."

"Well, Regie, you certainly *do* say *the* most *sing*ular things," said Mr. Clerke.

But that was a speech he often made, with the emphasis as it is given here.

## CHAPTER XXII

## NURSE BUNDLE FINDS A VOCATION—RAGGED ROBIN'S WIFE—MRS. BUNDLE'S IDEAS ON HUSBANDS AND PUBLIC-HOUSES

I was very happy under Mr. Clerke's sway, and yet I was glad to go to school.

The tutor himself, who had been "on the foundation" at Eton, had helped to fill me with anticipations of public-school life. It was decided that I also should go to Eton, but as an oppidan, and becoming already a partisan of my own part of the school, I often now disputed conclusions or questioned facts in my tutor's school anecdotes, which commonly tended to the sole glorification of the "collegers."

I must not omit to mention an interview that about this period took place between my father and Mrs. Bundle. It was one morning just after the Eton matter had been settled, that my nurse presented herself in my father's library, her face fatter and redder than usual from being swollen and inflamed by weeping.

"Well?" said my father, looking up pleasantly from his accounts. But he added hastily, "Why, bless me, Mrs. Bundle, what is the matter?"

"Asking your pardon for troubling you, sir," Nurse Bundle began in a choky voice, "but as you made no mention of it yourself, sir, your kindness being what it is, and the young gentleman as good as gone to school, and me eating the bread of idleness ever since that tutor come, I wished to know, sir, when you thought of giving me notice."

"Give you notice to do what?" asked my father.

"To leave your service, sir," said Mrs. Bundle, steadily. "There's no nurse wanted in this establishment now, sir."

My father laid one hand on Mrs. Bundle's shoulder, and with the other he drew forward a miniature of my mother which always hung on a standing frame on the writing-table.

"It is like yourself to be so scrupulous," he said; "but you will never again speak of leaving us, Mrs. Bundle. Please, for her sake," added my father, his own voice faltering as he looked towards the miniature. As for Nurse Bundle, her tears utterly forbade her to get out a word.

"If you have too much to do," my father went on, "let a young girl be got to relieve you of any work that troubles you; or, if you very much wish for a home to yourself, I have no right to refuse that, though I wish you could be happy under my roof, and I will see about one of those cottages near the gate. But you will not desert me—and Reginald—after so many years."

"The day I do leave will be the breaking of my heart," sobbed Nurse Bundle, "and if there was any ways in which I could be useful—but take wages for nothing, I could not, sir."

"Mrs. Bundle," said my father, "if your wages were a matter of any importance to me, if I could not afford even to pay you for your work, I should still ask you to share my home, with such comforts as I had to offer, and to help me so far as you could, for the sake of the past. I must always be under an obligation to you which I can never repay," added my father, in his rather elaborate style. "And as to being useful, well, ahem, if you will kindly continue to superintend and repair my linen and Master Reginald's—"

"Why, bless your innocence, sir, and meaning no disrespect," said Mrs. Bundle, "but there ain't no mending in *your* linen. There was some darning in the tutor's socks, but you give away half-a-dozen pair last Monday, sir, as hadn't a darn in 'em no bigger than a pea."

I think it was the allusion to "giving away" that suggested an idea to my father in his perplexity for employing Nurse Bundle.

"Stay," he exclaimed, "Mrs. Bundle, there is a way in which you could be of the greatest service to me. I often feel that the loss of a lady at the head of my household must be especially felt among the poor people around us— additionally so, as Mr. Andrewes is not married, and there is no lady either at the Rectory or here to visit the sick and encourage the mothers and children. I fear that when I do anything for them it is often in a wrong way, or for wrong objects."

"Well, sir," said Mrs. Bundle, an old grievance rushing to her mind, "I had thought myself of making so bold as to speak to you about that there Tommy Masden as you give half-crowns to, as tells you one big lie on the top of another, and his father drinks every penny he earns, and his mother at the back-door all along for scraps, and throwed the Christmas soup to the pig, and said they wasn't come to the workus yet; and a coat as good as new of yours, sir, hanging out of the door of the pawnshop, and giving me such a turn I thought my legs would never have carried me home, till I found you'd given it to that Tommy, who won't do a hand's turn for sixpence, but begs at every house in the parish every week as comes round, and tells everybody, as he tells yourself, sir, that he never gets nothing from nobody."

"Well, well," said my father, laughing, "you see how I want somebody to look out the real cases of distress and deserving poverty. Of course, I must speak to Mr. Andrewes first, Mrs. Bundle, but I am sure he will be as glad as myself that you should do what we have neither of us a wife to undertake."

I know Nurse Bundle was only too glad to reconcile her honest conscience to staying at Dacrefield; and I think the allusion to the lack of a lady head to our household decided her at all risks to remove that reason for a second Mrs. Dacre. Moreover, the duties proposed for her suited her tastes to a shade.

Mr. Andrewes was delighted. And thus it came about that, though my father would have been horrified at the idea of employing a Sister of Mercy, and though Bible-woman and district visitor were names not familiar in our simple parochial machinery, Mrs. Bundle did the work of all three to the great benefit of our poor neighbours.

Not, however, to the satisfaction of those who had hitherto leant most upon the charity of the Hall. A certain picturesquely tattered man, living at some distance from the village, who was in the habit of waylaying my father at certain points on the estate, with well-timed agricultural remarks and a cunning affectation of half-wittedness and good-humour, got henceforward no half-crowns for his pains.

"Mrs. Bundle has knocked off all my pensioners," my father

would laughingly complain. But he was quite willing that the half-crowns should now be taken direct to the man's wife and children, instead of passing from his hands to the public-house. "Though really the good woman—for I understand she is a most excellent person—is singularly hard-favoured," my father added, "and looks more as if she thrashed old Ragged Robin than as if he beat her, as I hear he does."

"Nothing inside, and the poker outside, makes a many women as they've no wish to sit for their picter," said Mrs. Bundle, severely, in reply to some remark of mine, reflecting, like my father's, on the said woman's appearance. "And when a woman has children, and their father brings home nothing but kicks and bad language, in all reason if it isn't the death or the ruin of her, it makes her as she 'asn't much time nor spirits to spare for dropping curtseys and telling long tales like some people as is always scrap-seeking at gentry's back-doors. But I knows a clean place when I takes it unawares, and clothes with more patch than stuff, and all the colour washed out of them, and bruises hid, and a bad husband made the best of, and children as knows how to behave themselves."

The warmth of Mrs. Bundle's feelings only prompted me to tease her; and it was chiefly for "the fun of working her up" that I said—

"Ah, but, Nurse, you know we heard she went after him one night to the public-house, and made a row before everybody. I don't mean he ought to go to the public-house, but still, I'm sure if I'd a wife who came and hunted me up when she thought I ought to be indoors, I'd—well, I'd try and teach her to stay at home. Besides, women ought to be gentle, and perhaps if she were sweeter-tempered with him, he'd be kinder to her."

"Do you know what she went for, Master Reginald?" said Nurse Bundle. "Not a halfpenny does he give her to feed the children with, and everything in that house that's got she gets by washing. And the rich folk she washed for kept her waiting for her money—more shame to 'em; there was weeks run on, and she borrowed a bit, and pawned a bit, and when she went the day they said they'd pay her, he'd been before and drawed the money, and was drinking it up when she went to see if she could get any, and then laughed at her, and sent her back to the children as was starving, and the neighbour she'd borrowed of as called her a thief and threatened to have her up. Gentle! why, bless your innocence, who ever knowed gentleness do good to a drunkard? She should have stood up to him sooner, and he'd never have got so bad. She's kept his brute ways to herself and made his home comfortable with her own earnings, till he thinks he may do anything and never bring in nothing. She did lay out some of his behaviour before him that day, and he beat her for it afterwards. But if it had been me, Master Reginald, I'd have had money to feed them children, or I'd have fought him while I'd a bit of breath in my body."

And with all my respect for Nurse Bundle, I am bound to say that I think she would have been as good as her word.

"Go to your tutor, my dear," she continued, "and talk Latin and Greek and such like, as you knows about; but don't talk rubbish about pretty looks and ways for a woman as is tied to a drunkard, for I can't abear it. I seed enough of husbands and public-houses in my young days to keep me a single woman and my own missis. Not but what I've had my feelings like other folk, and plenty of offers, besides a young cabinet-maker as had high wages and the beautifullest complexion you ever saw. But he was overfond of company; so I went to service, and cried myself to sleep every night for three months; and when next I see him he was staggering along the street, and I says, 'I'm sorry to see you like this, William,' and he says, 'It's your doing, Mary; your No's drove me to the glass.' And I says, 'Then it's best as it is. If one No drove you to the glass, you and married life wouldn't suit, for there's plenty of Noes there.' So I left him wiping his eyes, for he always cried when he was in beer. And I says to myself, 'I'll go back to place, where I knows what I'm working for, and can leave it if we don't suit.' And it was always the same, my dear. If it was a nice-looking footman, he'd have his evening out and come home fresh; and if it was an elderly butler as had put a little by, he wanted to set up in the public line. So I kept myself to myself, my dear, for I'm short-tempered at the best, and could never put up with the abuse of a man in liquor."

I was so thoroughly converted to the side of Ragged Robin's wife, that I at once pressed some of my charity money on Mrs. Bundle for her benefit; but I tried to dispute my nurse's unfavourable view of husbands by instancing her worthy brother-in-law at Oakford.

"Ah, yes, Buckle," said Mrs. Bundle, in a tone which seemed to do less justice to the saddler's good qualities than they deserved. "He's a good, soft, easy body, is Buckle."

Whence I concluded that Mrs. Bundle, like some other ladies, was not altogether easy to please.

I think it was during our last walk through the village before Mr. Clerke left us, that he and I called on Ragged Robin's wife. She was thankful, but not communicative, and the eyes, deep set in her bony and discoloured face, seemed to have lost the power of lighting up with hope.

"My dear Regie," said Mr. Clerke, as we turned homewards, "I never saw anything more pitiable than the look in that woman's eyes; and the tone in which she said, 'There be a better world afore us all, sir—I'll be well off then,' when I said I hoped she'd be better off and happier now, quite went to my heart. I'm afraid she never will have much comfort in this world, unless she outlives her lord and master. Do you know, Regie, she reminds me very much of an ill-treated donkey; her bones look so battered, and there's a sort of stubborn hopelessness about her like some poor Neddy who is thwacked and tugged this way and that, work he never so hard. Poor thing, she may well look forward to Heaven," added my tutor, whose kind heart was very sore on this subject, "and it's a blessed thought how it will make up, even for such a life here!"

"What will make it up to the donkeys?" I asked, taking Mr. Clerke at a disadvantage on that standing subject of dispute between us—a "better world" for beasts.

But my tutor only said, "My dear Regie, you *do* say *the* most *sin*gular things!" which, as I pointed out, was no argument, one way or another.

Meanwhile, through Mrs. Bundle, we did our best for Robin's wife and certain other ill-treated women about the place. Mrs. Bundle could be very severe on the dirt and discomfort which "drove some men to the public as would stay at home if there was a clean kitchen to stay in, and less of that nagging at a man and screaming after children as never made a decent husband nor a well-behaved child yet." Yet in certain cases of undeserved brutality, like Robin's, I fear she sometimes counselled resistance, on the principle that it "couldn't make him do worse, and might make him do better."

I am sure that my father had never thought of Mrs. Bundle acting as sick nurse in the village; but matters seemed to develop of themselves. She was so experienced and capable that she could hardly fail to smoothe the disordered bed-clothes, open the window, clear the room of the shiftless gossips who flocked like ravens to predict death, and take the control of mismanaged sick-rooms. It came to be a common thing that some wan child should present itself at our door with the message that "Missis Bundle she wants her things, for as mother be so bad, she says she'll see her over the night."

As for herself, I doubt if she had ever been happier in her life. Her conscience was at ease, for she certainly worked hard enough for her wages, and it was good to see the glow of pleasure that an oft-repeated remark of my father's never failed to bring over her honest face.

"Don't overwork yourself, Mrs. Bundle. What should we do if you were laid up?"

# CHAPTER XXIII

## I GO TO ETON—MY MASTER—
## I SERVE HIM WELL

I went joyfully to school the first time, but each succeeding half with less and less willingness. And yet my school-days were very happy ones, especially to look back upon.

"You will be in the same tutor's house as Lionel Damer," said my father; "and I have written to ask him to befriend you."

"Just the sort of idiotic thing parents do do," said Sir Lionel, on our first meeting. "You may thank your stars I don't pay you off for it."

Leo had grown much taller since we met, but he had lost none of his beauty. I was overpowered by his noble appearance and the air of authority he wore, and then and there gave him the hero-worship of my heart. It was with a thrill of delight that I heard him add, "However, I want a fag, and I dare say I can take you. Any sock with you?"

"Oh, yes, Leo," said I, hastily; "a big hamper. And there are two cakes, and a pigeon pie, and lots of jam, and some macaroons and turnovers, and two bottles of raspberry vinegar."

"My name's Damer," said Leo. "Can you cook?"

"Not yet, Damer," said I, hoping that my answer conveyed my willingness to learn. For I was quite prepared for all the duties of fag life from Mr. Clerke's descriptions. And I was prepared to perform them, pending the time when I should have a fag of my own.

I must do Leo justice. His tyranny was merciful. I was soon expert in preparing his breakfast. I used to fetch him hot dishes from the shop. My own cooking was not good, and I made, so he said, the most execrable coffee, which led him to fling the contents of the pot at me one morning, ruining my shirt, trickling hot and wet down my body under my clothes, and giving me infinite trouble in cleaning his carpet. (As to *his* coffee, and the salad dressing he made, and his cooking generally, when he chose to do it, I have never met with anything like it since. However, things taste well in one's school-days.)

Leo Damer was one of those people who seem able to do everything just a little better than his neighbours, without attaining overwhelming superiority in any one line. The masters always complained that he did not do as much in school as he might have done, and yet he stood well with them. His conduct was of the highest. I may say here that, knowing him intimately in boyhood and youth, I am able to assert that his moral conduct was always "without reproach." His own freedom from vice, and the tight hand he kept over me, who lived but to admire and imitate him, were of such benefit to me in the manifold temptations of school-life as I can never forget. His self-respect amounted to self-esteem, his love for other people's good opinion to a failing, he was refined to fastidiousness; but I think these characteristics helped him towards the exceptional character he bore. A keen sensitiveness to pain and discomfort, and considerable natural indolence, further tended to keep him out of scrapes into which an adventurous spirit led many more reckless boys. He had never been flogged, and he said he never would be. "I would drown myself sooner," he said to me. And if any dark touch were wanting to complete my hero's portrait, it was given by this terrible threat, in which I put full faith.

He was a dandy, and his dressing-table was the plague of my life. Well do I remember breaking some invaluable toilette preparation on it, and the fit of rage in which he flung the broken bottle at my head. He was very sorry when his first wrath was past, and he bound up my head, and gave me a pound of sausages, and a superbly bound copy of Young's "Night Thoughts," which I still possess. I also retain a white scar above one of my eyes, in common with at least eight out of every ten men I know.

"Do you ever hear from your cousin?" Sir Lionel asked one day in careless tones.

"Polly writes to me sometimes," said I.

"You can show me the next letter you get," said Sir Lionel condescendingly; which I accordingly did, and thenceforward he saw all my letters from her. I was soon clever enough to discover that Leo liked to be asked after by his old friends, and to receive messages from them, which led me to write to Polly, begging her always to send "nice messages" to Sir Lionel, as he would then treat me well, and perhaps give me some of his smoked bacon for breakfast. Her reply was characteristic:

"MY DEAR REGIE,—"

I shan't send nice messages to Leo. I am sorry you showed him the letter where I said he was handsome. Handsome is that handsome does, and if he treats you badly he is very ugly, and I hate him. If he doesn't give you any bacon, he's very mean. You may tell him what I say.

"I am your affectionate cousin,

"POLLY."

I was obliged to hide this letter from Leo; but when he asked me if I had heard from Polly I could not lie to him, and he sent me to Coventry for withholding the letter. I bore a day and a half of his silence and neglect; then I could endure it no longer, and showed him the letter. He was less angry than I expected. He coloured and laughed, and called me a little fool for writing such stuff to Polly, and said her answer was just like her. Then he gave me some of the bacon, and we were good friends again.

But the seal of our friendship was a certain occasion when I saved him from the only flogging with which he was ever threatened.

He was unjustly believed to be concerned in an insolent breach of certain orders, and was sentenced to a flogging which was really the due of another lad whom he was too proud to betray. He would not even condescend to remonstrate with the boy who was meanly allowing him to suffer, and betrayed his anguish in the matter so little that I doubt if the real culprit (who never was a week unflogged himself) had any idea what the punishment was to poor Leo.

He hid himself from us all; but in the evening I got into his room, where I found him, pale and silent, putting some things into a little bag.

"Little one!" he cried, "I know you can keep a secret. I want you to help me off. I'm going to run away."

"Oh Damer!" I cried; "but supposing you're caught; it'll be much worse then."

"They won't catch me," he said, his lip quivering. "I can disguise myself. And I shall never come back till I'm a man. My guardian would bring me here again. He thinks a man can hardly be a gentleman unless he was well flogged in his youth. Look here old fellow, I've left everything here to you. Keep out of mischief as I've shown you how, and—and—you'll tell Polly I wasn't to blame."

I was now weeping bitterly. "Dear Damer," said I, "you can't disguise yourself. Anybody would know you; you're too good-looking. Damer," I added abruptly, "did you ever pray for things? I used to at home, and do you know, they always came true. Wait for me, I'll be back soon," I concluded, and rushing to my room, I flung myself on my knees, and prayed with all my heart for the averting of this, to my young mind, terrible tragedy. I dared not stay long, not knowing what Leo might do, and on the stairs I met the real culprit, who was in our house. To this day I remember with amusement the flood of speech with which, in my excitement, I overwhelmed him. I painted his meanness in the darkest colours, and the universal contempt of his friends. I made him a hero if he took his burden on his own back. I dwelt forcibly on Leo's bitter distress and superior generosity. I bribed him to confess all with my many-weaponed pocket-knife (the envy of the house). I darkly hinted a threat of "blabbing" myself, as my meanness in telling tales would be as nothing to his in allowing Leo to suffer for his fault. Which argument prevailed I shall never know. I fancy Leo's distress and the knife did it between them, for he was both good-natured and greedy. He told the truth by a great effort, and took his flogging with complete indifference.

Thenceforward Leo and I were as brothers. He taught me to sketch, we kept divers pets together, and fused our botanical collections. He cooked unparalleled dishes for us, and read poetry aloud to me with an exquisite justness and delicacy of taste that I have never heard surpassed.

His praise was nectar to me. When he said, "I tell you what, Regie, you've an uncommon lot of general information, I can tell you," my head was quite turned. Whatever he did seemed right to me. When I first came to school, my hat was duly peppered and pickled by the boys and replaced by me with one of unexceptionable shape. My shirts then gave offence to my new master.

"I suppose,' he said, surveying me deliberately, "a good many of your things are made by Mrs. Baggage?"

"Nurse Bundle makes my shirts, Damer," said I.

"It's all the same," said Damer. "I knew it was connected with a *parcel* somehow. Well, the *Package* patterns are very pretty, no doubt, but I think it's time you were properly rigged out."

Which was duly done; and when holidays came and the scandalized Mrs. Bundle asked what I had done "with them bran-new fine linen shirts," and where "them rubbishing cotton rags" had come from that I brought in their place, I could only inform her, with a feeble imitation of Leo's lofty coolness, that I had used the first to clean Damer's lamp, and that the second were the "correct thing."

One day I said to him, "I don't know why, Damer, but you always make me think of a vision of one of the Greek heroes when I see you walking in the playing-fields."

I believe my simply-spoken compliment deeply gratified him; but he only said, like Mr. Clerke, "You *do* say the oddest things, little 'un!"

# CHAPTER XXIV

## COLLECTIONS—LEO'S LETTER—
## NURSE BUNDLE AND SIR LIONEL

If Nurse Bundle hoped that when I went to school an end would be put to the "collections" which troubled her tidy mind, she was much deceived. Neither Leo nor I were bookworms, and we were not by any means so devoted as some boys to games and athletics. But for collections of all kinds we had a fancy that almost amounted to mania.

Our natural history manias in their respective directions came upon us like fevers. We "sickened" at the sight of somebody else's collection, or because we had been reading about butterflies, or birds' eggs, or water-plants, as the case might be. When "the complaint" was "at its height," we lived only for specimens; we gave up leisure, sleep, and pocket-money to our collection; we made notes and memoranda in our grammars and lexicons that had no classical reference. We sent letters to country newspapers which never appeared, and asked questions that met with no reply. We were apt, also, to recover from these attacks, leaving Nurse Bundle burdened with boxes or folios of dry, dusty broken fragments of plants and insects, which we did not touch, but which she was strictly forbidden to destroy. We pursued our fancies during the holidays. I have now a letter that I got from

Damer after my fourth half:

"London.

"MY DEAR REGIE,—

"*Eureka*! What do you think? My poor governor collected moths. I bullied my guardian till he let me have the collection. Such specimens! No end of foreign ones we know nothing about, and I am having a case made. I found a little book with his notes in. We are quite at sea to go flaring about with nets and bruising the specimens. The way is to dig for chrysalises. Mind you do; and how I envy you! For I have to be in this horrid town, when I long to be grubbing at the roots of trees. Polly quite agrees with me. She hates London; and says the happiest time in her life was when she was at Dacrefield. My only comfort is to go to the old bookstalls and look for books about moths and butterflies. Imagine! The other day when your aunt was out, I took Polly with me. She said she would give anything on earth to go. So we went. We went into some awful streets, and had some oysters at a stall, and came back carrying no end of books; and just as we got in at the door there were your aunt and Lady Chelmsfield coming out. What a rage your aunt was in! I tried to take all the blame, but she shut Polly up for a fortnight. It's a beastly shame, but Polly says the expedition was worth it; her spirit is splendid. I never wrote such a long letter in my life before, but I am in the blues, and have no one to talk to. I wish my poor governor had lived. I wish I were in the country. I wish your aunt was a moth. Wouldn't I pin her to a cork! Mind you work up old Mother Hubbard to a sumptuous provision of grub for next half, and don't forget the other grubs. Would that I could dig with thee for them. *Vale*!

"Thine ever,

"LIONEL DAMER."

Of course this ended in Leo's being invited to Dacrefield. He came, and, wonderful to relate, we got Polly too. My father invited her and my aunt to visit us, and they came. As Leo said, Aunt Maria "behaved better than we expected." Indeed, Leo had no reason to complain of her treatment of him as a rule, for he was constantly at the Ascotts' house during his holidays.

And so we rambled and scrambled about together, Leo, and Polly, and I. And we added largely to our collections, and made a fernery (the Rector helping us), and rode about the country, and were thoroughly happy. We generally went to the nursery for a short time before dressing for dinner, where we teased and coaxed Mrs. Bundle, and ate large slices of an excellent species of gingerbread called "parliament," which she kept in a tin case in the cupboard. In return for these we entertained her with marvellous "tales of school," rousing her indignation by terrible narratives of tyrannous and cruel fagging, and taking away her breath by tales of reckless daring, amusing impudence, or wanton destructiveness common to boys. Some of these we afterwards confessed to be fables, told—as we politely put it—to "see how much she *would* swallow."

After dinner we were expected to sit with my father and Aunt Maria in the drawing-room. Then, also, poor Polly was expected to "give us a little music," and dutifully went through some performances which were certainly a remarkable example of how much can be acquired in the way of mechanical musical skill where a real feeling for the art is absent. After politely offering to turn over the leaves of her music, which Polly always declined (it was the key-note of her energetic character that she "liked to do everything herself"), my father generally fell asleep. I whiled away the time by playing with Rubens under the table, Aunt Maria "superintended" the music in a way that must have made any less stolid performer nervous, and Leo was apt to try and distract Polly's attention by grimaces and pantomime of a far from respectful nature behind Aunt Maria's back.

Sir Lionel was not a favourite with Nurse Bundle. I was unfortunate enough to give her a prejudice against him, which nothing seemed to wear out. Thinking his real, or affected mistake about her name a good joke, and having myself the strongest relish and admiration for his school-boy wit, I had told Nurse Bundle of his various versions of her name; and had tried to convey to her the comic nature of the scenes when my hat was pickled, and when Leo condemned my home-made shirts.

But quite in vain. Nurse Bundle's sense of humour (if she had any) was not moved by the things that touched mine. She looked upon the destruction of the hat and the shirts as "a sinful waste," and as to Leo's jokes—

"Called me a baggage, did he?" said the indignant Mrs. Bundle. "I'll Sir Lionel him when I get the chance. At my time of life, too!"

And no explanation from me amended matters. By the time that Leo did come, Nurse Bundle had somewhat recovered from the insult, but he was never a favourite with her. He "chaffed" her freely, and Mrs. Bundle liked to be treated with respect. Still there was a fascination about his beauty and his jokes against which even she was not always proof. I have seen her laugh and fetch out the parliament box when Leo followed her about like a dog walking on its hind legs, wagging an old piece of rope at the end of his jacket for a tail, and singing—

"Good Mother Hubbard,
Pray what's in your cupboard?
Could you give a poor dog a bone?"

And when he got the parliament he would "sit up" and balance a slice of the gingerbread on his nose, till Polly and I cheered with delight, and Rubens became frantic at the mockery of his own performances, and Mrs. Bundle complained that "Sir Lionel never knowed when to let nonsense be."

But I think she was something like the housemaid who "did the bedrooms," and who complained bitterly of the additional trouble given by Leo and me when we were at Dacrefield, and who was equally pathetic about the dulness of the Hall when we returned to school. "The young gentlemen be a deal of trouble, but they do keep a bit of life in the place, sure enough."

# CHAPTER XXV

## THE DEATH OF RUBENS—POLLY'S NEWS
## —LAST TIMES

When one has reached a certain age time seems to go very fast. Then, also, one begins to understand the meaning of such terms as "the uncertainty of life," "changes," "loss of friends," "partings," "old times," etc., which ring sadly in the ears of grown-up folk.

After my first half at Eton, this universal experience became mine. There was never a holiday time that I did not find some change; and, too often, a loss to meet my return.

One of the first and bitterest was the death of Rubens.

I had been most anxious to get home, and yet somehow, in less high spirits than usual, which made it feel not unnatural that my father's face should be so unusually grave when he came to meet me.

"I have some very bad news for you, my dear boy," he said. "I fear, Regie, that poor Rubens is dying."

"He've been a-dying all day, sir," said the groom, when we stood at last by Rubens' side. "But he seems as if he couldn't go peaceable till you was come."

He seemed to be gone. The beautiful curls were limp and tangled. He lay on his side with his legs stretched out; his eyes were closed. But when I stooped over him and cried "Ruby!" his flabby ears pricked, and he began to struggle.

"It's a fit," said the groom.

But it was nothing of the kind. Rubens knew what he was about, and at last actually got on to his feet, when, after swaying feebly about for a moment, he staggered in my direction (he could not see) and literally fell into my arms, with one last wag of his dear tail.

"They say care killed the cat," said Mrs. Bundle, when I went up to the nursery, "but if it could cure a dog, my deary, your dog would have been alive now. I never see the Squire so put about since you had the fever. He was up at five o'clock this very morning, the groom says, putting stuff into the corners of its mouth with a silver teaspoon, and he've had all the cow doctors about to see him, and Dr. Gilpin himself he've been every day, and Mr. Andrewes the same. And I'd like to know, my deary, what more could be done for a sick Christian than the doctor and parson with him daily till he dies?"

"A Christian would be buried in the churchyard," said I; "and I wish poor dear Rubens could."

But as he couldn't, I made his grave where the churchyard wall skirted the grounds of the Hall. "Perhaps, some day, the churchyard will have to be enlarged," I explained to the Rector, who was puzzled by my choice of a burying-place, "and then Rubens will *get taken in*."

My father was most anxious to get me another pet. I might have had a dog of any kind. Dogs of priceless breeds, dogs for sporting, for ratting, and for petting; dogs for use or for ornament. From a bloodhound and mastiff almost large enough for me to ride, to a toy poodle that would go into my pocket—I might have chosen a worthy successor to Rubens, but I could not.

"I shall never care for any other dog," I was rash enough to declare. But my resolve melted away one day at the sight of a soft, black ball, like a lump of soot, which arrived in a game-bag, and proved to be a retriever pup. He grew into a charming dog, of much wisdom and amiability. I called him Sweep.

Thus half by half, holidays by holidays, changes, ceaseless changes went on. Births, deaths, and marriages furnished my father with "news" for his letters when I was away, and Nurse Bundle and me with gossip when I came back.

I heard also at intervals from Polly. Uncle Ascott's wealth increased yearly. The girls grew up. Helen "was becoming Tractarian and peculiar," which annoyed Aunt Maria exceedingly. Mr. Clerke had got a curacy in London, and preached very earnest sermons, which Aunt Maria hoped would do Helen good. Mr. Clerke worked very hard, and seemed to like it; but he said that his happiest days were Dacrefield days. "I quite agree with him," Polly added. Then came a letter:—"Oh, my dear Regie, fancy! Miss Blomfield is married. And to whom, do you think? Do you remember the old gentleman who sent us the cinder-parcel? Well, it's to him; and he is really a very jolly old man; and thinks there is no one in the world like Miss Blomfield. He told her he had been carefully observing her conduct in the affairs of daily life for eight years. My dear Regie, *fancy* waiting eight years for one's next door neighbour, when one was quite old to begin with! You have no idea how much younger and better she looks in a home of her own, and a handsome silk dress. Can you fancy her always apologising for being so happy? She thinks she has too much happiness, and is idle, and who knows what. It makes me feel quite ill, Regie, for if she is idle, and has too much happiness, what am I, and what have I had? Do you remember the days when you proposed that we should be very religious? I am sure it's the only way to be very happy: I mean happy *always*, and *underneath*. Leo says the great mistake is being *too* religious, and that people ought to keep out of extremes, and not make themselves ridiculous. But I think he's wrong. For it seems just to be all the heap of people who are only a little religious who never get any good out of it. It isn't enough to make them happy whatever happens, and it's just enough to make them uncomfortable if they play cards on a Sunday. I know I wish I were really good, like Miss Blomfield, and Mr. Clerke, and Helen. * * *"

It was the year of Miss Blomfield's marriage that Ragged Robin's wife died. We had all quite looked forward to the peace she would enjoy when she was a widow, for it was known that delirium tremens was surely shortening her husband's life. But she died before him. Her children were wonderfully provided for. They were girls, and we had them all at the Hall by turns in some sort of sub-kitchenmaid capacity, from which they progressed to higher offices, and all became first-class servants, and "did well."

"My dear," said Nurse Bundle, "there ain't no difficulty in finding homes for gals that have been brought up to clean, and to do as they're bid. It's folk as can't do a thing if you set it 'em, nor take care of a thing if you gives it 'em, as there's no providing for."

I almost shrink from recording the hardest, bitterest loss that those changeful years of my school-life brought me—the death of Mr. Andrewes. It was during my holidays, and yet I was not with him when he died.

I do not think I had noticed anything unusual about him beforehand. He had not been very well for some months, but we thought little of it, and he never dwelt upon it himself. I was in the fifth form at the time, and almost grown up. Sweep was a middle-aged dog, the wisest and handsomest of his race. The Rector always dined with us on Sunday, but one evening he excused himself, saying he felt too unwell to come out, and would prefer to stay quietly at home, especially as he had a journey before him; for he was going the next day to visit his brother in Yorkshire for a change. But he asked if my father would spare me to come down and spend the evening with him instead. I rightly considered Sweep as included in the invitation, and we went together.

As we went up the drive (so familiar to me and poor little Rubens!) I thought I had never seen the Rector's garden in richer beauty, or heard such a chorus from the birds he loved and protected. Indeed the border plants were luxuriant almost to disorder. It struck me that Mr. Andrewes had not been gardening for some time. Perhaps this idea led me to notice how ill he looked when I went indoors. But dinner seemed to revive him, and then in the warm summer sunset we strolled outside again. The Rector leant heavily on my arm. He made some joke about my height, I remember. (I was proud of having grown so tall, and secretly thought well of my general appearance in the tail-coat of "fifth form.") With one arm I supported Mr. Andrewes, the other hung at my side, into the hand of which Sweep ever and anon thrust his nose caressingly.

"How well the garden looks!" I said. "And your birds are giving you a farewell concert."

"Ah! You think so too?" said the Rector, quickly.

I was puzzled. "You are going to-morrow, are you not?" I said.

"Yes, of course. I see," said the Rector laughing. "I was thinking of a longer journey. How superstitions do cling to north-countrymen! We've a terrible lot of Paganism in us yet, for all the Christians that we are!"

"What was your superstition just now?" said I.

"Oh, just part of a belief in the occult sympathy of the animal world with humanity, which, indeed, I am by no means prepared to give up."

"I should think not!" said I.

"Though doubtless the idea that they feel and presage impending death to man must be counted a fable."

"Awful rot!" was my comment. "I say, sir, I'm sure you're not well, to get such stuff into your head."

"It's just that," said the Rector. "When I was a boy, I was far from strong, and being rather bookish, I was constantly overworking my head. What weird fancies and fads I had then, to be sure! I was haunted by a lot of nervous plagues which it's best not to explain to people who have never been tormented with them. One of the least annoying was a sensation which now and then took possession of me that everything I saw, heard, or did, was 'for the last time.' I've often run back down a lane to get another glimpse of home, and done over again something I had just finished—to break the charm! The old childish folly has been plaguing me the last few days. It is strong on me to-night."

"Then we'll talk of something else," said I.

Eventually our conversation became a religious one. It was like the old days before I went to school. We had not had much religious talk of late years. To say the truth, since I became an Eton man the religious fervour of my childhood had died out. A strong belief in the practical power of prayer (especially "when everything else failed") was almost all that remained of that resolution to which Polly had alluded in her letter. In discussions with her, I took Leo's view of the subject. I warned her in a common-sense way against being "religious overmuch" (not that I had any definite religious measure in my mind); I laughed at Helen; I indulged a little cheap wit, and made Polly furious, by smart sneers about women and parsons. I puzzled her with scraps of old philosophy, and theological difficulties of venerable standing, and was as proud to discomfit her faith as if my own soul had no stake in the matter. I fairly drove her to tears about the origin of evil. Sometimes I would have "Sunday talks" with her in a different spirit, but even then she said I "did her no good," for I would not believe that she could "have anything to repent of."

I fancy Mr. Andrewes had asked me to come to him that evening greatly for the purpose of having a "Sunday talk." My father had wished me to be confirmed at home rather than at school, and as Bishops did not hold confirmations at such short intervals then as they do now, an opportunity had only just occurred. Mr. Andrewes was preparing me, and it was a great annoyance to him that his ill-health obliged him to go away in the middle of his instructions. I think he was feverish that night. Every now and then he spoke so rapidly that I could hardly follow him. Then there were pauses in which he seemed lost, and abrupt changes of subject, as if he could hardly control the order of his thoughts. And in all the evident strain and anxiety to say everything that he wished to say to me appeared that morbid fancy of its being "the last time."

After we had talked for some time he said, "Life goes wonderfully fast, Regie, though you may not think so just now. I do so well remember being a child myself. I was eight years old, I think, when I prayed for money enough to buy a *Fuchsia coccinea* (they had not been in England more than ten or twelve years then). My brother gave me half-a-crown, and I got one. It seems as if that one yonder must be it. I began a model of my father's house in card-board one winter, too. Then I got bronchitis, and did not finish it. I have been intending to finish it ever since, but it lies uncompleted in a box upstairs. So we purpose and neglect, till death comes like a nurse to take us to bed, and finds our tasks unfinished, and takes away our toys!"

Presently he went on: "Our mechanical arbitrary division of time is indeed a very false one. See how one day drags along, and how quickly another passes. The true measure of time is that which makes each man's life a day, his day. The real night is that in which no man can work. Indeed, nothing can be more true and natural than those Eastern expressions. I remember things that happened in my childhood as one remembers what one did this morning. What a lot of things I meant to do to-day! And one runs out into the garden instead of setting to work, and it is noon before one knows where he is, and other people take up one's time, and the afternoon slips away, and a man's day had need be fifty times its length for him to do all he means and ought to do, and to run after all the distractions the devil sends him as well. So comes old age, the evening when one is tired, and it's hard to make any fresh start; and then we're pretty near the end, at 'the last feather of the shuttle,' as we say in Yorkshire. I often think that the pitiful shortness of this life, compared with a man's hopes and plans, is almost proof enough of itself that there must be another, better fitted to his aims and capacities. And then—measure the folly of not securing *that*! And talking of proofs, Regie, and whilst I'm taking the privilege of this season of your confirmation to proffer a little advice, above all things make up your mind as to what you believe, and on what grounds you believe it. Ask yourself, my boy, if you believe the articles of the Apostles' Creed to be real positive truths. Do you think there is evidence for the facts, as matters of history? Are you ever likely to have the time or the talent to test this for yourself? And, if not, do you consider the authority of those who have done so, and staked everything upon their truth, as sufficient? Will you receive it as the Creed of your Church? Make up your mind, my boy, above all things make up your mind! Have *some* convictions, some real opinions, some worthy hopes; and be loyal to, and in earnest about, whatever you do pin your faith to, I assure you that vagueness of faith affects people's every-day conduct more than they think. The sort of belief which takes a man to church on Sunday who would be ashamed to look as if he were really praying, or confessing real sins when he gets there, is small help to him when the will balances between right and wrong. It is truly, as a matter of mere common sense, a poor bargain, a wretched speculation, to be half religious; to get a few checks and scruples out of it, and no real strength and peace; and, it may be, to lose a man's soul, and not even gain the world. For who dare promise himself that Christ our Judge, who spent a self-denying human youth as our example, and so loved us as to die for us, will accept a youth of indifference, and a dissatisfied death-bed on our part? And if it be all true, and if gratitude and common sense, and self-preservation, and the example and advice of great men, demand that we shall serve GOD with all our powers, don't you think the devil must, so to speak, laugh in his sleeve to see us really conceited of being too large-minded to attend too closely, or to begin to attend too early, to our own best interests?"

"Ah!" he added after a while, "my dear boy—dearer to me than you can tell—the truth is, I covet for you the unutterable blessing of a youth given to GOD. What that is, some know, and many a man converted late in life has imagined with heart-wrung envy: an Augustine, already numbered with the Saints, a Prodigal robed and decked with more than pardon, haunted yet by dark shadows of the past, the husks and the swine. My boy, with an unstained youth yet before you to mould as you will, get to yourself the elder son's portion— 'Thou art ever with Me, and all that I have is thine.' And what GOD has for those who abide with Him, even here, who can describe? It's worth trying for, lad; it would be worth trying for, on the chance of GOD fulfilling His promises, if His Word were an open question. How well worth any effort, any struggle, you'll know when you stand where I stand to-night."

We had reached the front steps of the house as he said this. The last few sentences had been spoken in jerks, and he seemed alarmingly feeble. I shrank from understanding what he meant by his last words, though I knew he did not refer to the actual spot on which we stood. The garden was black now in the gloaming. The reflection from the yellow light left by the sunset in the west gave an unearthly brightness to his face, and I fancied something more than common in the voice with which he quoted:

"Jesu, spes poenitentibus,
Quam pius es petentibus!
Quam bonus te quaerentibus!
*Sed quid invenientibus*!"

But I was fanciful that Sunday, or his nervous "fads" were infectious ones; for on me also the superstition was strong to-night that it was "the last time."

# CHAPTER XXVI

## I HEAR FROM MR. JONATHAN ANDREWES—YORKSHIRE—ALATHEA *alias* BETTY—WE BURY OUR DEAD OUT OF OUR SIGHT—VOICES OF THE NORTH

I sat up for a short time with my father on my return. When I went to bed, to my amazement Sweep was absent, and I could not find him anywhere. I did not like to return to the Rectory, for fear of disturbing Mr. Andrewes' rest, so I went to bed without my dog.

I was up early next morning, for I had resolved to go to the station to see Mr. Andrewes off, though his train was an early one, that I might disabuse him of his superstition by our meeting once more. It was with a secret sense of relief, for my own part, that I saw him arranging his luggage. Sweep, by-the-by, had turned up to breakfast, and was with me.

"I've come to see you off," I shouted, "and to break the charm of *last times*, and Sweep has come too."

"Strange to say, Sweep came back to me last night, after you left," said the Rector, laughing; "and he added omen to superstition by sitting under the window when I turned him out, and howling like a Banshee."

Juliana Horatia Ewing

Sweep himself looked rather foolish as he wagged his tail in answer to the Rector's greeting. He had the air of saying, "We were all a little excited last night. Let it pass."

For my own part I felt quite reassured. The Rector was in his sunniest mood, and as he watched us from the window to the very last, his face was so bright with smiles, that he hardly looked ill.

For some days Sweep and I were absent, fishing.

When I returned, I found on my mantelpiece a black-edged letter in an unfamiliar hand. But for the black I should have fancied it was a bill. The writing was what is called "commercial." I opened it and read as follows:

"North Side Mills, Blackford,

Yorks. 4/8, 18—.

"SIR,

"I have to announce the lamented Decease of my Brother—Reverend Reginald Andrewes, M.A.—which took place on the 3rd inst. (3.35 A.M.), at Oak Mount, Blackford; where a rough Hospitality will be very much at your Service, should you purpose to attend the Funeral. Deceased expressed a wish that you should follow the remains; and should your respected Father think of accompanying you, the Compliment will give much pleasure to Survivors.

"Funeral party to leave Oak Mount at 4 P.M. on Thursday next (the 8th inst.), D.V.

"A line to say when you may be expected will enable me

to meet you, and oblige,

"Yours respectfully,

"JONATHAN ANDREWES.

"Reginald Dacre, Esq., Jun."

It is useless to dwell upon the bitterness of this blow. My father felt it as much as I did, and neither he nor I ever found this loss repaired. One loses some few friends in a lifetime whose places are never filled.

We went to the funeral. Had the cause of our journey been less sad, I should certainly have enjoyed it very much. The railway ran through some beautiful scenery, but it was the long coach journey at the end which won my admiration for the Rector's native county. I had never seen anything like these noble hills, these grand slopes of moorland stretching away on each side of us as we drove through a valley to which the river running with us gave its name. Not a quiet, sluggish river, keeping flat pastures green, reflecting straight lines of pollard willows, and constantly flowing past gay villas and country cottages, but a pretty, brawling river with a stony bed, now yellow with iron, and now brown with peat, for long distances running its solitary race between the hills, but made useful here and there by ugly mills built upon the banks. Sometimes there was a hamlet as well as a mill. Tracts of the neighbouring moorland were enclosed and cultivated, the fields being divided by stone walls, which looked rude and strange enough to us. The cottages were also built of stone; but as we drove through a village I could see, through several open doors, that the rooms were very clean and most comfortably furnished, though without carpets, the floors, like everything else, being of stone.

It was dark before we reached Blackford. The latter part of our journey was through a coal and iron district, and the glare of the furnace fires among the hills was like nothing I had ever seen. At the coach office we were met by Mr. Jonathan Andrewes. He was a tall, well-made man, with badly-fitting clothes, rather tumbled linen, imperfectly brushed hair and hat, and some want of that fresh cleanliness and finish of general appearance which went to my idea of a gentleman's outside. I found him a warm-hearted, cold-mannered man, with a clear, strong head, and a shrewdness of observation which recalled the Rector to my mind more than once. The tones of his voice made me start sometimes, they were so like the voice that I could never hear again in this life. He spoke always in the broad dialect into which the Rector was only wont to relapse in moments of excitement.

A carriage, better appointed than the owner, and a man-servant rather less so, were waiting, and took us to Oak Mount. In the hall our host apologized for the absence of Mrs. Andrewes, who was at the sea-side, out of health.

"But Betty 'll do her best to make you comfortable, sir," he said to my father, and turning to a middle-aged woman with a hard-featured, sensible face, and very golden hair tightly braided to her head, who was already busy with our luggage, he added, "You've got something for us to eat, Betty, I suppose?"

"T' supper 'll be ready by you're ready for it," said Betty, when she had finished her orders to the man who was taking our things upstairs. "But when folks is come off on a journey, they'll be glad to wash their 'ands, and I've took hot water into both their rooms."

The maid's familiarity startled me. Moreover, I fancied that for some reason she was angry, judging by the form and manner of her reply; but I have since learned that the ordinary answers of Scotch and Yorkshire folk are apt to sound more like retorts than replies.

In the end I became very friendly with this good woman. Her real name, I discovered, was not Betty. "They call me Alathea," she said, meaning that that was her name, "but I've allus gone by the name of Betty." From her I learnt all the particulars of my dear friend's last illness, which I never should have got from the brother.

"He talked a deal about you," she said. "But you see, you're just about t' age his son would have been if he'd lived."

"His son!" I cried: "was Mr. Andrewes married?"

"Ay," said she, "Master Reginald were married going i' two year. It were his wife's death made him that queer while he couldn't abide the business, and he'd allus been a great scholard, so he went for a parson."

Every detail that I could get from Alathea was interesting to me. Apart from the sadly interesting subject, she had admirable powers of narration. Her language (when it did not become too local for my comprehension) was forcible and racy to a degree, and she was not checked by the reserve which clogged Mr. Jonathan's lips. The following morning she came to the door of the drawing-room (a large dreary room, which, like the rest of the house, was handsomely *upholstered* rather than furnished), and beckoned mysteriously to me from the door. I went out to her.

"You'd like to see the body afore they fastens it up?" she said.

I bent my head and followed her.

"He makes a beautiful corpse," she whispered, as we passed into the room. It was an incongruous remark, and stirred again an hysterical feeling that had been driving me to laugh when I felt most sad amid all the grotesquely dreary preparations for the "burying." But, like some other sayings that offend ears polite, it had the merit of truth.

It was not the beauty of the Rector's face in death, however, noble as it was, that alone drew from me a cry of admiration when I stooped over his coffin. From the feet to the breast, utterly hiding the grave clothes, and tastefully grouped about his last pillow, were the most beautiful exotic flowers I ever beheld. Flowers lately introduced that I had never seen, flowers that I knew to be rare, almost priceless—flowers of gorgeous colours and delicate hothouse beauty, lay there in profusion.

"Mr. Jonathan sent for 'em," Betty murmured in my ear. "There's pounds and pounds' worth lies there. He give orders accordingly. There warn't to be a flower 'at warn't worth its weight in gowd a'most. Mr. Reginald were that fond of flowers."

I made no answer. Bitterly ached my heart to think of that dear and noble face buried out of sight; the familiar countenance that should light up no more at the sight of me and Sweep. "He looks so happy," I muttered, almost jealously. Alathea laid her hand upon my arm.

"Them that sleeps in Jesus rests well, my dear. And, as I said to Master Jonathan this morning, it ain't fit to overbegrudge them 'ats gone Home."

I think it was the naming of that Name, in which alone we vanquish the bitter victories of death, that recalled the verse which had been floating in my head ever since that evening at the Rectory:

"Jesu, spes poenitentibus,
Quam pius es petentibus!
Quam bonus te quaerentibus!
*Sed quid invenientibus*!"

The loneliness of my childhood had given me a habit of talking to myself. I did not know that I had quoted that verse of the old hymn aloud, till I discovered the fact from hearing afterwards, to my no small surprise, that Betty had reported that I "made a beautiful prayer over the corpse."

\* \* \* \* \*

The grim and hideous pomp of the funeral was most oppressive, though in the abundance of plumes and mutes Mr. Jonathan had, as in the more graceful tribute of the flowers, honoured his brother nobly after his manner, which was a commercial one. It was a very expensive "burying." Alathea did tell me what "the gin and whiskey for the mourners alone come to," though I have forgotten. But we lost sight of the ignoble features of the occasion when the sublime office for the Burial of the Dead began. When it was ended I understood one of Betty's brusque remarks, which had puzzled me when it came out at breakfast-time.

"You'll 'ave to take what ye can get for your dinners, gentlemen," she had said; "for the singers is to meet at three, and I can't pretend to do more nor I can."

The women mourners at the funeral (there were a few) all wore large black silk hoods, which completely disguised them; but at the end of the service one of them pushed hers back, and I recognized the golden hair of Alathea, as she joined a group rather formally collected on one side of the grave. She looked round as if to see that all were ready, and then in such a soprano voice as one seldom hears, she "started" the funeral hymn. It was the Old Psalm—

"O GOD, our help in ages past,
Our hope for years to come;

Our shelter from life's stormy blast,
And our eternal home."

I had heard very little chorus-singing of any kind; and I did not then know that for the best I had heard—that of St. George's choir at Windsor—voices were systematically imported from this particular district. My experience of village singing was confined to the thin nasal unison psalmody of our school children, and an occasional rustic stave from a farmer at an agricultural dinner. Great, then, was my astonishment when the little group broke into the four-part harmony of a fine chorale. One rarely hears such voices. Betty had a grand soprano, and on the edge of the group stood a little lad singing like a bird, in an alto of such sweet pathos as would have made him famous in any cathedral choir.

Mr. Jonathan's head drooped lower and lower. Affecting as the hymn was in my ears, it had for him, no doubt, associations I could not share. My father moved near him, with an impulse of respectful sympathy.

To me that one rich voice of harmony spoke as the voice of my old teacher; and I longed to cry to him in return, "I have made up my mind. It *is* worth trying for! It is 'worth any effort, any struggle.' Our eternal home!"

# CHAPTER XXVII

## THE NEW RECTOR—AUNT MARIA TRIES TO FIND HIM A WIFE—MY FATHER HAS A SIMILAR CARE FOR ME

The stone that marks the burying-place of the Andrewes family taught me the secret of the special love the Rector bore me. It recorded the deaths of his wife Margaret, and of his son Reginald. The child was born in the same year as myself.

Mr. Jonathan Andrewes came to Dacrefield on business connected with his brother's affairs, and he accepted my father's hospitality at the Hall. We seldom met afterwards, and were never intimate; but, slight as it was, our tie was that of friendship rather than acquaintance.

The next presentation to the Rectory of Dacrefield was in my father's gift. He held it alternately with the Bishop, to whom he owed Mr. Andrewes. He gave it to my old tutor.

Mr. Clerke's appointment had the rare merit of pleasing everybody. After he had been settled with us for some weeks, my father said,

"Mr. Clerke is good enough to be grateful to me for

presenting him to the living, but I do not know how to be grateful enough to him for accepting it. I really cannot think how I should have endured to see Andrewes' place filled by some new broom sweeping away every trace of our dear friend and his ways. Clerke's good taste in the matter is most delicate, most admirable, and very pleasant to my feelings."

The truth is there was not a truer mourner for the old Rector than the new one. "I so little thought I should never see him again," he cried to me. "I have often felt I did not half avail myself of the privilege of knowing such a man, when I was here. I have notes of more than a score of matters, on which I purposed to ask his good counsel, when we should meet again. And now it will never be."

"I feel so unworthy to fill his place," he would say. "My only comfort is in trying to carry out all his plans, and, so far as I can, tread in his steps."

In this spirit the new Rector followed the old one, even to becoming an expert gardener. He bought the old furniture of the Rectory. Altogether, we were spared those rude evidences of change which are not the least painful parts of such a loss as ours.

With the parishioners, I am convinced, that Mr. Clerke was more popular than Mr. Andrewes had been. They liked him at first for his reverence for the memory of a pastor they had loved well. I think he persuaded them, too, that there never could be another Rector equal to Mr. Andrewes. But in reality I believe he was himself more acceptable. He was much less able, but also less eccentric and reserved. He was nearer to the mental calibre of his flock, and not above entering into parish gossip after a discreet fashion. He was not less zealous than his predecessor.

When Aunt Maria came to visit us she gladly renewed acquaintance with Mr. Clerke, who was a great favourite of hers. I think she imagined that he was presented to Dacrefield on the strength of her approval. She used to say to me, "You know Reginald, I always told your father that Mr. Clerke was a most spiritual preacher." But after seeing him as Rector of Dacrefield, she added, "He's getting much too 'high.' Quite like that extraordinary creature you had here before. But it's always the way with young men."

Uncle Ascott did not publicly undertake Mr. Clerke's defence, but he told me:

"I don't pretend to understand these matters as Maria does, but I can tell you I never liked any of our London parsons as I like Clerke. There's something I respect beyond anything in the feeling he has for your late Rector. And between ourselves, my dear boy, I rather like a nicely-conducted service."

So Uncle Ascott and Mr. Clerke were the very best of friends, and my uncle would go to the Rectory for a quiet smoke, and was always hospitably received. (Neither my aunt nor my father liked the smell of tobacco.) Aunt Maria's favour was a little withdrawn. She tried a delicate remonstrance, but though he was most courteous, it was not to be mistaken that the Rector of Dacrefield meant to go his own way: "the way of a better man than I shall ever be," he said. Failing to change his principles, or guide his practice, my aunt next became anxious to find him a wife. "Medical men and country parsons ought to be married," said she, "and it will settle him."

She selected a young lady of the neighbourhood, the daughter of a medical man. "Most suitable," said my aunt (by which she meant not *quite* up to the standard she would have exacted for a son of her own), "and with a little money." She patronised this young lady, and even took her with us one day to lunch at the Rectory; but when she said something to Mr. Clerke on the subject, she found him utterly obdurate. "What does he expect, I wonder?" cried my aunt, rather unfairly, for the Rector had not given utterance to any matrimonial hopes. She always said, "She never could feel that Mr. Clerke had behaved well to poor Letitia Ramsay," which used to make downright Polly very indignant. "He didn't behave badly to her. It was mamma who always took her everywhere where he was; and how she could stand it, I don't know! He never flirted with her, Regie."

The next few years of my life seemed to whirl by. They were very happy ones. My dear father lived, and our mutual affection only grew stronger as time went on.

Then, when I was a man, it gradually dawned upon me, through many hints, that my father had the same anxiety for me that Aunt Maria had had for the Rector. He wished me to marry. At one time or another my fancy had been taken by pretty girls, some of whom were unsuitable in every respect but prettiness, and some of whom failed to return my admiration. My dear father would not have dreamed of urging on me a marriage against my inclinations, but he would have preferred a lady with some fortune as his daughter-in-law.

"Our family is an old one, my dear boy," he said, "but the estate is much smaller than it was in my great-grandfather's time. Don't suppose that I would have you marry for money alone; but if the lady should be well portioned, sir, so much the better—so much the better."

At last he seemed to set his heart upon my having one of Aunt Maria's daughters. People who live years and years on their own country estates without going much from home are apt sometimes to fancy that there is nothing like their own family circle. My father had a great objection, too, to what he called "modern young ladies." I think he thought that, as there was no girl left in the world like my poor mother, I should be safer and happier with one of my cousins. They were unexceptionably brought up, and would all have considerable fortunes.

But though I was very fond of my cousins, I had no wish to choose a wife from them. They had been more like sisters to me than cousins from our childhood. At one time, it is true, I was rather sentimental about Helen. She was the only one of the sisters who was positively pretty, and her resolute character and unusual tastes roused a romantic interest in me for a while. When she was twelve years old, she was found one day by Aunt Maria in the bedroom of a servant who had fallen ill, and to whom she was attending with the utmost dexterity. She had a genius for the duties of a sick room, which developed as she grew up. There were no lady-doctors then, but Helen was determined to be a hospital nurse. Strongly did Aunt Maria object, and Helen never defied her wishes in the matter. But she had all Mrs. Ascott's determination, with more patience. She waited long, but she followed her vocation at last.

None of the other girls had any special tastes. The laborious and expensive education of their childhood did not lead to anything worth the name of a pursuit, much less a hobby, with any one of them. Of the happiness of learning, of the exciting interest of an intellectual hobby, they knew nothing. With much pains and labour they had been drilled in arts and sciences, in languages and "the usual branches of an English education." But, apart from social duties and amusements, the chief occupation of their lives was needlework. I have known many people who never received proper instruction in music or drawing, who yet, from what they picked up of either art by their own industry and intelligence, nearly doubled the happiness of their daily lives. But in vain had "the first masters" made my cousins glib in chromatic passages, and dexterous with tricks of effects in colours and crayons. They played duets after dinner, and Aunt Maria sometimes showed off the water-colour copies of their school-room days, which, indeed, they now and then recopied for bazaars; but for their own pleasure they never touched a note or a pencil. Perhaps real enjoyment only comes with what one has, to a great extent, taught oneself. Helen had been her own mistress in the art of nursing, and it was an all-absorbing interest to her.

They were very nice girls, and I do not think were entirely to blame for the small use to which they put their "advantages." They were tall and lady-like, aquiline-nosed and pleasant-looking, without actual beauty. It took a wonderful quantity of tarlatan to get them ready for a ball, a large carriage to hold them, and a small amount of fun to make them talkative and happy.

Except Maria, they all inherited my aunt's firmness and decision of character. Maria, the oldest and largest, was the most yielding. She had more of Uncle Ascott about her.

## CHAPTER XXVIII

## I BELIEVE MYSELF TO BE BROKEN-HEARTED—MARIA IN LOVE—I MAKE AN OFFER OF MARRIAGE, WHICH IS NEITHER ACCEPTED NOR REFUSED

A phase of my life, into which I do not propose to enter, left me firmly resolved that (as I said in confidence to Clerke) "I shall marry to please the governor. One doesn't go in for a broken heart, you know, but it isn't in me to *care* a second time."

It was shortly after this that Maria and her mother came to stay at the Hall. A rather mysterious letter from my aunt had led to the invitation. It was for the benefit of Maria's health. My father also invited Polly; she was a favourite with him. Leo and some other friends were expected for shooting. Our neighbours' houses as well as ours were filling with visitors, and though I fancied myself a disappointed man, I found my spirits rising daily.

My aunt and Maria arrived first: Polly was visiting elsewhere, and was to join them in a day or two. I was glad to have ladies in the house again, and after dinner I strolled about the grounds with Maria. She was looking delicate, but it improved her appearance, and she quite pleased me by the interest she seemed to take in the place. But I had seen more of Maria during a visit I paid to London two months before than usual, and had been quite surprised to find her so well versed in Dacrefield matters.

"It's uncommonly pleasant having you here," said I, as we leaned over a low wall in the garden. "I wonder we do not become perfect barbarians, cut off as we are from ladies' society. I'm sure I wish you would settle down here instead of in London. You would civilise both the Rectory and the Hall."

I was really thinking of my uncle taking a house in the neighbourhood. I do not know what Maria was thinking of; but she looked up suddenly into my face, with a strange expression, as if half inclined to speak. She said nothing, however, only blushed deeply, and began walking towards the house. I puzzled for a few minutes over that pathetic look and blush, but I could make nothing of it, and it passed from my mind till the next evening after dinner, when, after a little ceremonious preamble, my father asked if there was "anything between" myself and my eldest cousin. In explanation of this vague question, he told me that Maria had been failing in health and spirits for some months; that my aunt's watchful observation and experience had led her to the conclusion that Maria was not in a consumption, but in love. As, however, she kept her own counsel, Mrs. Ascott could only guess in the matter. From her feverish interest in Dacrefield, her ill-concealed excitement when the visit was proposed, the improvement in her health since she came, and a multitude of other small facts which my aunt had ferreted out and patched together with an ingenuity that amazed me, Maria was supposed to care for me.

"We were a good deal together in town, sir," said I, "and Maria was very jolly with me. But I am sure I gave her no reason to think I was in love with her, and I don't believe she cares for me. It's one of my aunt's mare's nests, depend upon it. The poor girl has got a horrid cough, and, of course, she was pleased to get out of London smoke."

"If you did care for her," said my father; "and, above all, if you had led her to think you did, the course is obvious, and I have no doubt she would make an excellent wife. Polly is my favourite, and Maria is a year or two older than you. But she is a nice, sensible, well-bred woman. She is the eldest daughter, and will have—"

"My dear father," said I, "Maria and I are very friendly as cousins, but she has not an idea of me in any other than a brotherly relation. At least I think not," I added, for the look and blush that had puzzled me came back to my mind.

"I only mention this because I wished to warn you against trifling with your cousin's affections if you mean nothing," said my father.

"I should be sorry to trifle with any lady's affections, sir," was my reply. We said no more. I sighed, thinking of what I fully believed had blighted my existence. My father sighed, thinking, I know, of his own vain wish to see me happily married. At last I could bear it no longer, and calling Sweep, I went out into the garden. It was moonlight, and Maria was languidly pacing the terrace. I joined her, and we strolled away into the shrubbery.

I cannot say that my father's warning led me to shun Maria's society. My father and my aunt naturally talked together, and circumstances almost forced us two into *tete-a-tetes*. I could not fail to see that Maria liked to be with me, and I found the task of taking care of her soothing to what I believed to be my blighted feelings. We rode together (she had an admirable figure and rode well), and the exercise did her health great good. We often met Mr. Clerke in our rides, and he seemed to enjoy a canter with us, though he rode very little better than when I first knew him. We took long walks with Sweep, and from the oldest tenant to the latest puppy, everything about Dacrefield seemed to interest my fair cousin. I came at last to believe that Aunt Maria was right.

When I did come to believe it (and I do not think that any contemptible conceit made me hasty to do so), other thoughts followed. I was as firmly convinced as any other young man with my experiences that I could never again feel what I had felt for the person who shall be nameless. But the first bitterness of that agony being undoubtedly over, I felt that I might find a sober satisfaction in making my father's declining years happy by giving him a daughter-in-law, and that I was perhaps hardly justified in allowing Maria to fall into a consumption when I could prevent it. "There are some people," thought I, "with whom one could spend life very happily in a quiet fashion; people who would not offend one's taste, or greatly provoke one's temper, and whom one feels that one could please in like manner. *Suitable* people, in fact. And when a fellow has had his great heart-ache and it's all over, no doubt suitableness is the thing to make married life happy.... Maria is suitable."

I remember well the day I came to this conclusion. Our visitors had not yet arrived, but Polly was expected the next day, and Leo and some others shortly. "I may as well get it over before the house is full," I thought. But, to my vexation, I discovered that my father had asked Mr. Clerke to come up after dinner. "It's his own fault if I don't get another chance of speaking," thought I. But, as I strolled sullenly on the terrace (without Maria) a note arrived from the Rector to say that he was called away to see a sick man. I dashed into the drawing-room, gave the letter to my father, and seeing Maria was not there, I went on into the conservatory.

There are moments when even plain people look handsome. Notably when self-consciousness is quite absent, and some absorbing thought gives sentiment to the face, and grace and power to the figure. It was so at this moment with Maria, who stood gazing before her, the light from above falling artistically on her glossy hair and tall, elegant figure. At the sound of my footsteps she started, and the colour flooded her face as I came up to her. She sank on to a seat close by, as if too much agitated to stand.

"I have something I want to say to you," said I, stooping over her, and speaking in my gentlest voice. "May I say it?"

She moved her lips as if trying to speak, but there was no sound, and she just nodded her head, which then drooped so that I could hardly see her face.

"We have known each other since we were children," I began.

"Yes, Regie dear," murmured Maria.

"We were always very good friends, I think," continued I.

"Oh, yes, Regie dear."

"Childhood was a very happy time," said I, sentimentally.

"Oh, yes, Regie dear."

"But we can't be children for ever," I continued.

"Oh, no, Regie dear."

"Please take what I am going to say kindly, cousin, whatever you may think of it."

"Oh, yes, Regie dear."

"I hope I may truthfully say that your happiness is, as it ought to be, my chief aim in the matter."

Maria's response was inaudible.

"It's no good beating about the bush," said I, desperately clothing my sentiments in slang, after the manner of my age; "the fellow who gets you for a wife, Maria, must be uncommonly fortunate, and I hope that with a good husband, who made your wishes his first consideration, you would not be unhappy in married life yourself."

Lower and lower went her head, but still she was silent.

"You say nothing," I went on. "Probably I am altogether wrong, and you are too kind-hearted to tell me I am an impertinent puppy. It is Dacrefield—the place only—that you honour with your regard. You have no affection for—"

Maria did not let me finish this sentence. She put up her hands to stop me, and seemed as if she wished to speak; but after one pitiful glance she buried her face in her hands and wept bitterly. I am sure I have read somewhere that when a woman weeps she is won. So Maria was mine. I had a grim feeling about it which I cannot describe. "I hope the governor will be satisfied now," was my thought.

However, there is nothing I hate more than to see a woman cry. To be the means of making her cry is intolerable.

"Please, please, don't! Oh, Maria, what a brute you make me

feel. *Please* don't," I cried, and raising my cousin from her Niobe-like attitude, I comforted her as well as I could. She only said, "Oh, Regie dear, how kind you are," and laid her sleek head against my arm with an air of rest and trustfulness that touched my generosity to the quick. What right had I, after all, to accept an affection to which I could make no similar return? "However," thought I, "it's done now; and they say it's always more on one side than the other; and at least I'm a gentleman. I care for no one else, and she shall never know it was chiefly to please the governor. I suppose it will all come right."

Whilst I pondered, Maria had dried her eyes, and now sat up, gazing before her, almost in her old attitude.

"I wonder, Regie dear," she said, presently—"I wonder how you found out that I—that we—that I *cared*—"

"Oh, I don't know," said I, inanely, for I could not say that nothing could be plainer.

"I always used to think that to live in this neighbourhood would be paradise," murmured Maria, looking sentimentally but vacantly into a box of seedling balsams.

"I'm very glad you like it," said I. I could not make pretty speeches. An unpleasant conviction was stealing over my mind that I had been a fool, and had no one but myself to blame. I began to think that Maria would not have died of consumption even if I had not proposed to her, and to doubt if I were really so heartbroken as I had fancied. (Indeed the society of my cousin, who was a lady, had by this time gone far to cure me of my sentiment for one who was not, and who had been sensible enough to marry a man in her own rank of life, to my father's great relief, and, as I then thought, to my life-long disappointment.) The whole affair seemed a

Juliana Horatia Ewing

mockery, and I wished it were a dream. It was not thus that my father had plighted his troth to my fair mother. This was not the sort of affection that had made happy the short lives of Leo's parents. The lemon-scented verbena which I was pounding between my fingers bitterly recalled a little sketch of the monument to their memory which Leo had shown me in his Bible, where he had also pressed a sprig of verbena. Beneath the sketch he had written, "They were lovely and pleasant in their lives, and in death they were not divided." I remembered his telling me how young they were when they were married. How his father had never cared for any one else, and how he would like to do just the same, and marry the one lady of his love. I began, too, to think Clerke was right when he replied to my confidences, "I'm only afraid, Regie, that you don't know what love is."

It was whilst these thoughts were crowding all too vividly into my mind that Maria said, impressively, and with unmistakable clearness,

"After *all*, you know, Regie, he's a *thorough* gentleman, if he *is* poor. I must say *that*! And if he *has* a profession instead of being a landed proprietor, it's the *highest* and *noblest* profession there is."

It seemed to take away my breath. But I was standing almost behind Maria; she was preoccupied, and I had some presence of mind. I had opportunity to realize the fact that I was not the object of Maria's attachment, as I had supposed. I was not poor, I had no profession, and my common avocations did not, I fear, deserve to be called high or noble. The description in no way fitted me. Further still, it was evident that my cousin had not dreamed that I was making her an offer. She believed that I had discovered her attachment to some other man, and was grateful for my sympathy. I did not undeceive her. After a rapid review of the position, I said,

"But my dear Maria, though I have penetrated to the fact that you have a secret, and though I want beyond anything to help and comfort you, I do not yet know who the happy man is, remember."

"Don't you?" said Maria, looking up hastily, and the colour rushed to her face as before. "Oh, I thought you knew it was Mr. Clerke. You know, he *is* so good, and I've known him so long."

At this moment Aunt Maria's voice called from the drawing-room end of the conservatory.

"Will you give us a little music, Maria? Mr. Clerke has come after all, and Bowles has brought in the tea."

# CHAPTER XXIX

## THE FUTURE LADY DAMER—POLLY HAS A SECRET—UNDER THE MULBERRY-TREE

Polly came into the house, as she always did, like a sunbeam. Mrs. Bundle, who was getting old, and apt to be depressed in spirits from time to time, always revived when "Miss Mary" paid us a visit. A general look of welcome greeted her appearance in church on Sunday. My father made no secret of his pleasure in her society. I think she was in the secret of her sister's engagement, and Maria looked comforted by her coming.

Our meals were now quite merry. We had plenty of family gossip, and news of the neighbourhood to chat over.

"So Lady Damer that is to be is coming to the Towers," Maria announced at breakfast, on the authority of a letter she was reading. "Leo is coming here to shoot, isn't he, Regie?"

"We expect him every day," said I; "but I never knew he was engaged. Who is it?"

"Well, it's not an announced engagement," said Maria, "but everybody says it is to be. She is an heiress, and her father was an old friend of his guardian's. And, by-the-bye, Regie, her sister is coming too, and will do beautifully for you. She is co-heiress, you know. They're really very rich, and your one is lovely."

"I'm sure I'm very much obliged to you," said I, "and we are to dine at the Towers next week, so I shall see the heiresses. But suppose I take a fancy to the wrong one?"

"You can't have her," said Maria, laughing.

"I tell you she is for Leo, and she is very clever and strong-minded, which is just what he wants—a wife who can take care of him."

"Oh, deliver me from a strong-minded lady!" I cried. "Damer is quite welcome to her."

"Your one isn't a bit strong-minded," said Maria. "She is very pretty, but has no will of her own at all. She leans completely on Frances; I don't know what she'll do when she marries, for they have been orphans since they were quite children, and have never lived apart for a week."

At this point Polly broke in with even more warmth and directness of speech than usual,

"Frances Chislett is the most superior girl I ever knew. Men always laugh at strong-minded women; but I'm sure I don't know why. I can't think how any human being with duties and responsibilities can be either more useful or more agreeable for being weak-minded."

And this was all that Polly contributed to our nonsensical conversation about the heiresses.

After she came I forsook the society of Maria. I knew now

Juliana Horatia Ewing

that she only wanted to talk to me about the Rector and the parish. Besides, though Maria was strongly interested in Dacrefield for Clerke's sake, she knew much less of it than Polly, with whom I revisited numberless haunts of our childhood, the barns and stables, the fernery, the "Pulpit" and the "Pew."

I did not tell her of my romance with Maria. I was not proud of it. But as we sat together in the old apple-room above the stables, I confided to her my "unfortunate attachment," which I had now sufficiently recovered from not to be offended by her opinion, that it was all for the best that it had ended as it had.

I do not remember exactly how it was that I came to know that Polly—even Polly—had her own private heart-ache. I think I took an unfair advantage of her strict truthfulness, when I once suspected that she had a secret, and insisted upon her confiding in me as I had done in her. Nurse Bundle gave me the first hint. Mrs. Bundle, however, believed that "Miss Mary" was only waiting for me to ask her to be mistress of Dacrefield Hall. And though she had "never seen the young lady that was good enough for her boy," she graciously allowed that I might "do worse than marry Miss Mary."

"My time's pretty near come, my dear," said Mrs. Bundle, "but many's the time I pray the Lord to let me live to put in if it is but a pin, when your lady dresses for her wedding."

But I was not to be fooled a second time by the affectionate belief my friends had in my attractions.

"My dear old Nursey," said I, squatting down with Sweep by her easy chair, "I know what a dear girl Polly is, and if she wanted to be Mrs. Dacre she soon should be. But you're quite mistaken there; she is my dear sister, and always will be so, and never anything else."

"Well, well," said Nurse Bundle, "young folks know their own affairs better than the old ones, and the Lord above knows what's good for us all, but I'm a great age, and the Squire's not young, and taking the liberty to name us together, my deary, in all reason it would be a blessing to him and me to see you happy with a lady as fit to take your dear mother's place as Miss Mary is. For let alone everything else, my dear, servants is not what they used to be, and when I'm dead you'll be cheated out of house and home, without any one as knows what goes to the keeping of a family, and what don't."

"Well, Nursey," said I, "I'll try and find a lady to please you and the governor. But it won't be Polly, I know, and I wish it may be any one as good."

I bullied poor Polly sadly about having a secret, and not confiding it to me. She was far from expert at dissembling, and never told an untruth, so I soon drove her into a corner.

"I'm rather disappointed, I must confess, in one way," said I, having found her unable flatly to deny that she did "care for" somebody. "I always hoped, somehow, that you and Leo would make it up together."

"You heard what Maria said," said Polly, shortly.

"Oh, I don't believe in the heiress," said I, "unless you've refused him. He'd never take up with the blue-stocking lady and her money-bags if his old love would have had him."

"I wish you wouldn't call her names," said Polly, angrily. "I tell you she's the best girl I ever knew. I don't care much for most girls; they are so silly. I suppose you'll say that's envy, but I can't help it, it's true. But Frances Chislett never bores me. She only makes me ashamed of myself, and long to be like her. When she's with me I feel rough, and ignorant, and useless, and—"

"What a soothing companion!" I broke in.

"Poor Damer! So you want him to marry her, as one takes nasty medicine—all for his good."

"Want him to marry her!" repeated Polly, expressively. "No. But I am satisfied that he should marry *her*. So long as he is really happy, and his wife is worthy of him—and *she* is worthy of him—"

A light dawned upon me, and I interrupted her.

"Why, Polly, it *is* Leo that you care for!"

We were sitting under an old mulberry-tree near the gate, in the kitchen garden, but when I said this Polly jumped up and tried to run away. I caught her hand to detain her, and we were standing very much in the attitude of the couple in a certain sentimental print entitled "The Last Appeal," when the gate close by us opened, and my father put his head into the garden, shouting "James! James!" I dropped Polly's hand, and struck by the same idea, we both blushed ludicrously; for the girls knew as well as I did the plans made on our behalf by our respective parents.

"The men are at dinner, sir," said I, going towards my father. "Can I do anything?"

"Not at all—not at all; don't let me disturb you," said the old gentleman, with an unmistakably pleased expression of countenance. And turning to blushing Polly, he added in his most gracious tones,

"You look charming, my dear, standing under that old mulberry-tree, in your pretty dress. It was planted by my grandfather, your great-grandfather, my love, and Regie's also. I wish I could have you painted so. Quite a picture— quite a picture!"

Saying which, and waving off my attempts to follow him, he bowed himself out and shut the door behind him. When he had gone, Polly and I looked at each other, and then burst out laughing.

"The plot certainly thickens," said I, sitting down again. "I beg you to listen to the gratified parent whistling as he retires. What shall we do, Polly, how could you blush so?"

"How could I help it when I saw you get so red?" said Polly.

"We certainly are a wonderful family at this point," said I; "the whole lot of us in a mess with our love affairs, and my aunt and the governor off on completely wrong scents."

"Oh, I think everybody's the same," said Polly, picking off half-ripe mulberries and flinging them hither and thither; "but that doesn't make one any better pleased with oneself for being a fool."

"You're not a fool," said I, pulling her down to the seat again; "but I wish you wouldn't be cross when you're unhappy. Look at me. Disappointment has made me sympathetic instead of embittering me. But, seriously, Polly, I'm sure you and Leo will come all right, and in the general rejoicing your mother must let Clerke and poor Maria be happy. Even I might have found consolation with the beautiful heiress if I had been left to find out her merits for myself; but one gets rather tired of having young ladies suggested to one by attentive friends. The fact is, matrimony is not in my line. I feel awfully old. The governor is years younger than I am. Whoever saw *me* trouble *my* long legs and back to perform such a bow as he gave you just now? I wish he'd leave me in peace with Sweep. Since the day I came of age, when every old farmer in the place wound up his speech with something about the future Mrs. Reginald Dacre, I've had no quiet of my life for her. Clerke too! I really did think Clerke was a confirmed old bachelor, on ecclesiastical grounds. I wish I'd gone fishing to Norway. I wish a bit of the house would fall down. If the governor were busy with real brick and mortar, he wouldn't build so many castles in the air, perhaps."

As I growled, Sweep, beneath my feet, growled also. I believe it was sympathy, but lest it should be the approach of Aunt Maria (whom Sweep detested), Polly and I thought well to withdraw from the garden by another gate. We returned to the house, and I took her to my den to find a book to divert her thoughts. I was not surprised that a long search ended in her choosing a finely-bound copy of Young's "Night Thoughts."

"I often feel ashamed of knowing so little of our standard poets," she remarked parenthetically.

"Quite so," said I; "but I feel it right to mention that the marks in it are only mine."

# CHAPTER XXX

## I MEET THE HEIRESS—I FIND MYSELF MISTAKEN ON MANY POINTS—A NEW KNOT IN THE FAMILY COMPLICATIONS

Leo came to the Hall. "His" heiress came to the Towers, but not "mine." She was to follow shortly.

I could not make out how matters stood between Leo and Polly. When Damer came, Polly was three times as *brusque* with him as with any of us; he himself seemed dreamy, and just as usual.

We went to dine at the Towers. We were rather late. Leo, in right of his rank, took a dowager of position in to dinner. Our host led me across the room, and introduced me to "Miss Chislett."

She was not the sort of person I expected. It just flashed across me that I understood something of Polly's remark about Frances Chislett making her feel "rough." My cousins were ladies in every sense of the term, but Miss Chislett had a certain perfection of courteous grace and dignified refinement, in every word, and gesture, and attitude, as utterly natural to her as the vigorous tread of any barefooted peasant girl, and which one does meet with (but by no means invariably) among women of the highest class in England. Her dignity fell short of haughtiness (which is not high breeding, and is very easy of assumption); her grace and courtesy were the simple results of constant and skilful consideration for other people, and of a self-respect sufficient to dispense with self-consciousness. The advantage of wealth was evident in the exquisite taste and general effect of her costume. She was not beautiful, and yet I felt disposed for an angry argument with my cousins on the subject of her looks. Her head was nobly shaped, her figure was tall and beautiful, her grey eyes haunted one. I never took any lady to dinner who gave me so little trouble. When we had been together for two minutes, I felt as if I had known her for years.

"Well, what do you think of her?" said Polly, when we met in the drawing-room. Polly had been taken in by Mr. Clerke, and they had neither of them paid much attention to what the other was saying. Maria had said "yes" and "no" alternately to the observations of the elderly and Honourable Mr. Edward Glynn; but as he was deaf this mattered the less.

"Was I right?" said Polly.

"No," said I; "she's not a bit strong-minded." Polly laughed.

"I'll say one thing for her," said I; "I don't mind how often I take her in to dinner. She doesn't expect you to make conversation."

"Why, my dear Regie," said Polly, "you've been talking the whole of dinner-time!"

Leo had seated himself by the heiress. Poor Polly's eyes kept wandering towards them, and (I suppose, because I had heard so much about her) so did mine. It was only a quiet dinner-party, and Miss Chislett had brought out her needlework, some gossamer lace affair, and Leo leant over the sofa where she sat, playing with the contents of her workbox. Polly's eyes and mine were not the only ones turned towards them. Ours was not the only interest in the future Lady Damer.

Aunt Maria carried Polly off to the piano to "give us a little music," and I sat down and stultified myself with an album at the table, and Frances Chislett chatted with Sir Lionel. They were close by me, and every word they said was audible. It was the veriest chit-chat, and Leo's remarks on the little bunch of charms and knicknacks that he found in the workbox seemed trivial to foolishness. "I'd no idea Damer was so empty-headed," I thought, and I rather despised Miss Chislett for smiling at his feeble conversation.

"I often wonder what's the use of farthings," I heard him say as he turned one over in the bunch of knicknacks. "They won't buy anything (unless it's a box of matches). They only help tradesmen to cheat when they're 'selling off.'"

"I beg your pardon," said Miss Chislett, "I have bought most charming things for a farthing each."

"So have I," said I, turning round on my chair, and joining in the conversation, which seemed less purposeless after I began to take part in it. Leo looked at us both with a puzzled air.

"Frying-pans, for instance," said Miss Chislett.

"—and gridirons," said I.

"Plates, knives, and forks," said the heiress.

"—and flat irons," I concluded; playing involuntarily with the blob of lead which still hung at my watch-chain.

Polly had finished her performance, and was now standing near us. She understood the allusion, and laughed.

"Do *you* know what they're talking about?" asked Sir Lionel, going up to her. I sat down by the heiress.

"Were you ever at Oakford?" she asked, turning her grey eyes on me. She spoke almost abruptly, and with a touch of imperiousness that suddenly recalled to me where I had seen those eyes before.

"Certainly," said I, "and at the tinsmith's."

"What were you doing there?" she asked, and after all these years there was no mistaking the accent and gesture of the little lady of the grey beaver. Before she had well begun her apology for the question, I had answered it,

"BUYING A FLAT IRON FOR A FARTHING."

\* \* \* \* \*

"Well, you've gone it hard to-night, old fellow," said Damer, as we drove away from the Towers. "You and Miss Chislett will be county talk for six months to come."

"Nonsense," said I, "we knew each other years ago, and had a good deal to talk about."

But to Polly, as we parted for the night in the corridor, I said, "My dear child, to add to all the family complications, I'm head over ears in love with the future Lady Damer."

# CHAPTER XXXI

## MY LADY FRANCES—THE FUTURE LADY DAMER—WE UNDERSTAND EACH OTHER AT LAST

It was true. My theories and my disappointment went to the winds. We had few common acquaintances or social interests to talk about, and yet the time we spent together never seemed long enough for our fluent conversation. We had always a thousand things to say when we met, and feeling as if we had been together all our lives, I felt also utterly restless and wretched when I was not with her. Of course, I learnt her history. She and her sister were the little ladies I had seen in my childhood. The St. John family were their cousins, and as the boy, of whom mention has been made, did die in Madeira, the property eventually came to Frances Chislett and her sister. The estate was sold, and they were co-heiresses. Adeline, the other sister, soon came to the Towers. She was more like her old self than Frances. The exquisitely, strangely fair hair, the pale-blue eyes, the gentle helpless look, all were the same. She was very lovely, but Frances was like no other woman I had ever seen before, or have ever met with since. I resolved to ask Lionel Damer how matters really stood between them, and, if he were not engaged to her, to try my luck. One day when she was with us at the Hall I decided upon this. I was told that Lionel was in the library, and went to seek him. As I opened the door I saw him standing in front of Polly, who was standing also. He was speaking with an energy rare with him, and in a tone of voice quite strange to me.

"It's not like you to say what's not true," he was saying. "You are *not* well, you are *not* happy. You may deceive every one else, Polly, but you can never deceive me. All these years, ever since I first knew you—"

I stole out, shut the door, and went to seek Frances. I found her by Rubens' grave, and there we plighted our troth.

*     *     *     *     *

It was in the evening of the same day that Polly and I met in the hall, on our way to attempt the difficult task of dressing for dinner in five minutes. The grey-eyed lady of my love had just left me for the same purpose, and I was singing, I don't know what, at the top of my voice in pure blitheness of heart. Polly and I fairly rushed into each other's arms.

"My dear child!" said I, swinging her madly round, "I am delirious with delight, and so is Sweep, for she kissed his nose."

Poor Polly buried her head on my shoulder, saying,

"And, oh, Regie! I *am* so happy!"

It was thus that my father and Aunt Maria found us. Fate, spiteful at our happiness, had sent my father, stiff with an irreproachable neckcloth, and Aunt Maria, rustling in amber silk and black laces, towards the drawing-room, five minutes too early for dinner, but just in time to catch us in the most sentimental of attitudes, and to hear dear, candid, simple-hearted

Polly's outspoken confession—"I *am* so happy!"

"And how long are you going to keep your happiness to yourselves, young people?" said my father, whose face beamed with a satisfaction more sedately reflected in Aunt Maria's countenance. "Do you grudge the old folks a share? Eh, sir? eh?"

And the old gentleman pinched my shoulder, and clapped me on the back. He was positively playful.

"Stop, my dear father," said I, "you're mistaken."

"Eh, what?" said my father, and Aunt Maria drew her laces round her and prepared for war.

"Polly and I are not engaged, sir, if that's what you think," said I, desperately.

My father and Aunt Maria both opened their mouths at once.

"Dinner's on the table, sir," the butler announced. My father lacked a subject for his vexation, and turned upon old Bowles:

"Take the dinner to—"

"—the kitchen," said I, "and keep it warm for ten minutes; we are not ready. Now, my dear father, come to my room, for I have something to tell you."

There was no need for Polly to ask Aunt Maria to go with her. That lady drove her daughter before her to her bedroom, with a severity of aspect which puzzled and alarmed poor Leo, whom they passed in the corridor. A blind man could have told by the rustle of her dress that Mrs. Ascott would

Juliana Horatia Ewing

have a full explanation before she broke bread again at our table.

I fancy she was not severe upon the future Lady Damer, when Polly's tale was told.

As to my father, he was certainly vexed and put out at first. But day by day my lady-love won more and more of his heart. One evening, a week later, he disappeared mysteriously after dinner, and then returned to the dining-room, carrying some old morocco cases.

"My dear boy," he said, in an almost faltering voice, "I never dared to hope my dear wife's diamonds would be so worthily worn by yours. Your choice has made an old man very happy, sir. For a thoroughly high-bred tone, for intelligence, indeed, I may say, brilliancy of mind, and for every womanly grace and virtue, I have seen no one to approach her since your mother's death. I should have loved little Polly very much, but your choice has been a higher one—more refined—more refined. For, strictly between ourselves, my dear boy, our dear little Polly has, now and then, just a thought too much of your Aunt Maria about her."

The Rector and Maria were made happy. My father "carried it through," by my desire. Uncle Ascott was delighted, and became a benefactor to the parish; but it took Aunt Maria some years to forget that the patronised curate had scorned the wife she had provided for him, only to marry her own daughter.

When I bade farewell to Adeline on our wedding day, she gave me her cheek to kiss with a pretty grace, saying,

"You see, Regie, I *am* your sister after all!"

# CHAPTER XXXII

## WE COME HOME—MRS. BUNDLE
## QUITS SERVICE

The day my wife and I returned from our wedding trip to Dacrefield was a very happy one. We had a triumphal welcome from the tenants, my dear father was beaming, the Rector no less so, and good old Nurse Bundle showered blessings on the head of my bride.

Frances was a great favourite with her. She was devoted to the old woman, and her delicate tact made her adapt herself to all Mrs. Bundle's peculiarities. She sat with her in the nursery that night till nearly dinner-time.

"I must take her away, Nursey," said I, coming in; "she'll be late for dinner."

"Go with your husband, my dear," said Nurse Bundle, "and the Lord bless you both."

"I'll come back, Nursey," said Frances; "you'll soon see me again."

"Turn your face, my dear," said Nurse Bundle. "Hold up the candle, Master Reginald. Ay, ay, that'll do, my deary. I'll see you again."

We were still at dessert with my father, when Bowles came hastily into the room with a pale face, and went up to my wife.

"Did you send for Mrs. Bundle, ma'am, since you came down to dinner?" he asked.

"Oh, dear no," said my wife.

"Cook was going upstairs, and met Missis Bundle a little way out of her room," Bowles explained; "and Missis Bundle she says, 'Don't stop me,' says she, 'Mrs. Dacre wants me,' she says, and on she goes; and cook waits and waits in her room for her, and at last she comes down to me, and she says—"

"But where *is* Mrs. Bundle?" cried my father.

"That's circumstantially what nobody knows, sir," said Bowles with a distracted air.

We all three rushed upstairs. Mrs. Bundle was not to be found. My father was frantic; my wife with tears lamented that some chance word of hers might have led the half-childish old lady to fancy that she wanted her.

But a sudden conviction had seized upon me.

"You need not trouble yourself, my darling," said I; "you are not the Mrs. Dacre Nurse Bundle went to seek."

I ran to my father's dressing-room. It was as I thought.

Below my mother's portrait, on the spot where years before she had held me in her arms with tears, I, weeping also, held her now in mine—quite dead.

# Choose from Thousands of 1stWorldLibrary Classics By

A. M. Barnard
Ada Leverson
Adolphus William Ward
Aesop
Agatha Christie
Alexander Aaronsohn
Alexander Kielland
Alexandre Dumas
Alfred Gatty
Alfred Ollivant
Alice Duer Miller
Alice Turner Curtis
Alice Dunbar
Allen Chapman
Alleyne Ireland
Ambrose Bierce
Amelia E. Barr
Amory H. Bradford
Andrew Lang
Andrew McFarland Davis
Andy Adams
Angela Brazil
Anna Alice Chapin
Anna Sewell
Annie Besant
Annie Hamilton Donnell
Annie Payson Call
Annie Roe Carr
Annonaymous
Anton Chekhov
Archibald Lee Fletcher
Arnold Bennett
Arthur C. Benson
Arthur Conan Doyle
Arthur M. Winfield
Arthur Ransome
Arthur Schnitzler
Arthur Train
Atticus
B.H. Baden-Powell
B. M. Bower
B. C. Chatterjee
Baroness Emmuska Orczy
Baroness Orczy
Basil King
Bayard Taylor
Ben Macomber
Bertha Muzzy Bower
Bjornstjerne Bjornson

Booth Tarkington
Boyd Cable
Bram Stoker
C. Collodi
C. E. Orr
C. M. Ingleby
Carolyn Wells
Catherine Parr Traill
Charles A. Eastman
Charles Amory Beach
Charles Dickens
Charles Dudley Warner
Charles Farrar Browne
Charles Ives
Charles Kingsley
Charles Klein
Charles Hanson Towne
Charles Lathrop Pack
Charles Romyn Dake
Charles Whibley
Charles Willing Beale
Charlotte M. Braeme
Charlotte M. Yonge
Charlotte Perkins Stetson
Clair W. Hayes
Clarence Day Jr.
Clarence E. Mulford
Clemence Housman
Confucius
Coningsby Dawson
Cornelis DeWitt Wilcox
Cyril Burleigh
D. H. Lawrence
Daniel Defoe
David Garnett
Dinah Craik
Don Carlos Janes
Donald Keyhoe
Dorothy Kilner
Dougan Clark
Douglas Fairbanks
E. Nesbit
E. P. Roe
E. Phillips Oppenheim
E. S. Brooks
Earl Barnes
Edgar Rice Burroughs
Edith Van Dyne
Edith Wharton

Edward Everett Hale
Edward J. O'Biren
Edward S. Ellis
Edwin L. Arnold
Eleanor Atkins
Eleanor Hallowell Abbott
Eliot Gregory
Elizabeth Gaskell
Elizabeth McCracken
Elizabeth Von Arnim
Ellem Key
Emerson Hough
Emilie F. Carlen
Emily Bronte
Emily Dickinson
Enid Bagnold
Enilor Macartney Lane
Erasmus W. Jones
Ernie Howard Pie
Ethel May Dell
Ethel Turner
Ethel Watts Mumford
Eugene Sue
Eugenie Foa
Eugene Wood
Eustace Hale Ball
Evelyn Everett-green
Everard Cotes
F. H. Cheley
F. J. Cross
F. Marion Crawford
Fannie E. Newberry
Federick Austin Ogg
Ferdinand Ossendowski
Fergus Hume
Florence A. Kilpatrick
Fremont B. Deering
Francis Bacon
Francis Darwin
Frances Hodgson Burnett
Frances Parkinson Keyes
Frank Gee Patchin
Frank Harris
Frank Jewett Mather
Frank L. Packard
Frank V. Webster
Frederic Stewart Isham
Frederick Trevor Hill
Frederick Winslow Taylor

Friedrich Kerst
Friedrich Nietzsche
Fyodor Dostoyevsky
G.A. Henty
G.K. Chesterton
Gabrielle E. Jackson
Garrett P. Serviss
Gaston Leroux
George A. Warren
George Ade
Geroge Bernard Shaw
George Cary Eggleston
George Durston
George Ebers
George Eliot
George Gissing
George MacDonald
George Meredith
George Orwell
George Sylvester Viereck
George Tucker
George W. Cable
George Wharton James
Gertrude Atherton
Gordon Casserly
Grace E. King
Grace Gallatin
Grace Greenwood
Grant Allen
Guillermo A. Sherwell
Gulielma Zollinger
Gustav Flaubert
H. A. Cody
H. B. Irving
H.C. Bailey
H. G. Wells
H. H. Munro
H. Irving Hancock
H. R. Naylor
H. Rider Haggard
H. W. C. Davis
Haldeman Julius
Hall Caine
Hamilton Wright Mabie
Hans Christian Andersen
Harold Avery
Harold McGrath
Harriet Beecher Stowe
Harry Castlemon
Harry Coghill
Harry Houidini

Hayden Carruth
Helent Hunt Jackson
Helen Nicolay
Hendrik Conscience
Hendy David Thoreau
Henri Barbusse
Henrik Ibsen
Henry Adams
Henry Ford
Henry Frost
Henry James
Henry Jones Ford
Henry Seton Merriman
Henry W Longfellow
Herbert A. Giles
Herbert Carter
Herbert N. Casson
Herman Hesse
Hildegard G. Frey
Homer
Honore De Balzac
Horace B. Day
Horace Walpole
Horatio Alger Jr.
Howard Pyle
Howard R. Garis
Hugh Lofting
Hugh Walpole
Humphry Ward
Ian Maclaren
Inez Haynes Gillmore
Irving Bacheller
Isabel Cecilia Williams
Isabel Hornibrook
Israel Abrahams
Ivan Turgenev
J.G.Austin
J. Henri Fabre
J. M. Barrie
J. M. Walsh
J. Macdonald Oxley
J. R. Miller
J. S. Fletcher
J. S. Knowles
J. Storer Clouston
J. W. Duffield
Jack London
Jacob Abbott
James Allen
James Andrews
James Baldwin

James Branch Cabell
James DeMille
James Joyce
James Lane Allen
James Lane Allen
James Oliver Curwood
James Oppenheim
James Otis
James R. Driscoll
Jane Abbott
Jane Austen
Jane L. Stewart
Janet Aldridge
Jens Peter Jacobsen
Jerome K. Jerome
Jessie Graham Flower
John Buchan
John Burroughs
John Cournos
John F. Kennedy
John Gay
John Glasworthy
John Habberton
John Joy Bell
John Kendrick Bangs
John Milton
John Philip Sousa
John Taintor Foote
Jonas Lauritz Idemil Lie
Jonathan Swift
Joseph A. Altsheler
Joseph Carey
Joseph Conrad
Joseph E. Badger Jr
Joseph Hergesheimer
Joseph Jacobs
Jules Vernes
Julian Hawthrone
Julie A Lippmann
Justin Huntly McCarthy
Kakuzo Okakura
Karle Wilson Baker
Kate Chopin
Kenneth Grahame
Kenneth McGaffey
Kate Langley Bosher
Kate Langley Bosher
Katherine Cecil Thurston
Katherine Stokes
L. A. Abbot
L. T. Meade

L. Frank Baum
Latta Griswold
Laura Dent Crane
Laura Lee Hope
Laurence Housman
Lawrence Beasley
Leo Tolstoy
Leonid Andreyev
Lewis Carroll
Lewis Sperry Chafer
Lilian Bell
Lloyd Osbourne
Louis Hughes
Louis Joseph Vance
Louis Tracy
Louisa May Alcott
Lucy Fitch Perkins
Lucy Maud Montgomery
Luther Benson
Lydia Miller Middleton
Lyndon Orr
M. Corvus
M. H. Adams
Margaret E. Sangster
Margret Howth
Margaret Vandercook
Margaret W. Hungerford
Margret Penrose
Maria Edgeworth
Maria Thompson Daviess
Mariano Azuela
Marion Polk Angellotti
Mark Overton
Mark Twain
Mary Austin
Mary Catherine Crowley
Mary Cole
Mary Hastings Bradley
Mary Roberts Rinehart
Mary Rowlandson
M. Wollstonecraft Shelley
Maud Lindsay
Max Beerbohm
Myra Kelly
Nathaniel Hawthrone
Nicolo Machiavelli
O. F. Walton
Oscar Wilde

Owen Johnson
P.G. Wodehouse
Paul and Mabel Thorne
Paul G. Tomlinson
Paul Severing
Percy Brebner
Percy Keese Fitzhugh
Peter B. Kyne
Plato
Quincy Allen
R. Derby Holmes
R. L. Stevenson
R. S. Ball
Rabindranath Tagore
Rahul Alvares
Ralph Bonehill
Ralph Henry Barbour
Ralph Victor
Ralph Waldo Emmerson
Rene Descartes
Ray Cummings
Rex Beach
Rex E. Beach
Richard Harding Davis
Richard Jefferies
Richard Le Gallienne
Robert Barr
Robert Frost
Robert Gordon Anderson
Robert L. Drake
Robert Lansing
Robert Lynd
Robert Michael Ballantyne
Robert W. Chambers
Rosa Nouchette Carey
Rudyard Kipling
Saint Augustine
Samuel B. Allison
Samuel Hopkins Adams
Sarah Bernhardt
Sarah C. Hallowell
Selma Lagerlof
Sherwood Anderson
Sigmund Freud
Standish O'Grady
Stanley Weyman
Stella Benson
Stella M. Francis

Stephen Crane
Stewart Edward White
Stijn Streuvels
Swami Abhedananda
Swami Parmananda
T. S. Ackland
T. S. Arthur
The Princess Der Ling
Thomas A. Janvier
Thomas A Kempis
Thomas Anderton
Thomas Bailey Aldrich
Thomas Bulfinch
Thomas De Quincey
Thomas Dixon
Thomas H. Huxley
Thomas Hardy
Thomas More
Thornton W. Burgess
U. S. Grant
Upton Sinclair
Valentine Williams
Various Authors
Vaughan Kester
Victor Appleton
Victor G. Durham
Victoria Cross
Virginia Woolf
Wadsworth Camp
Walter Camp
Walter Scott
Washington Irving
Wilbur Lawton
Wilkie Collins
Willa Cather
Willard F. Baker
William Dean Howells
William le Queux
W. Makepeace Thackeray
William W. Walter
William Shakespeare
Winston Churchill
Yei Theodora Ozaki
Yogi Ramacharaka
Young E. Allison
Zane Grey